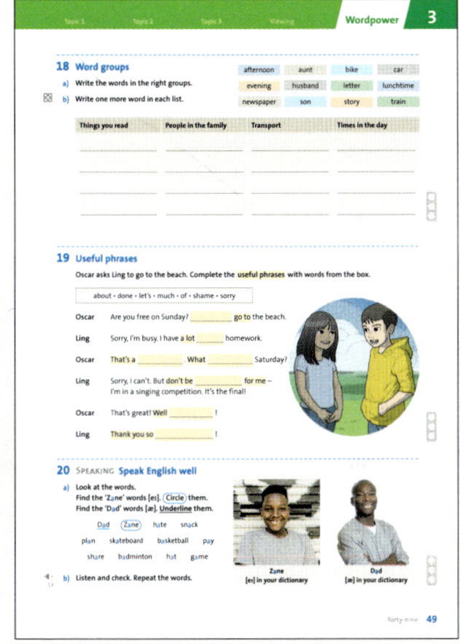

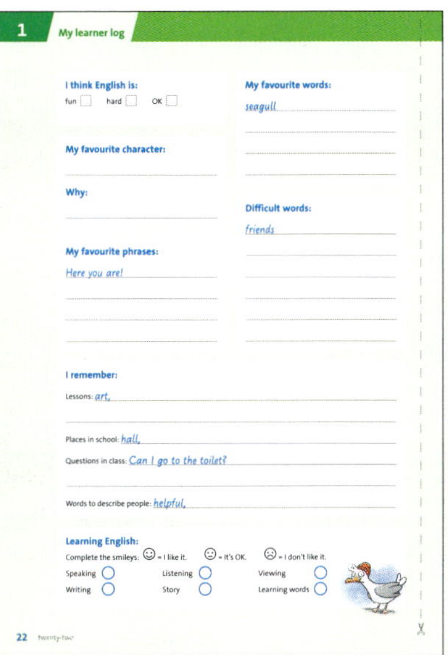

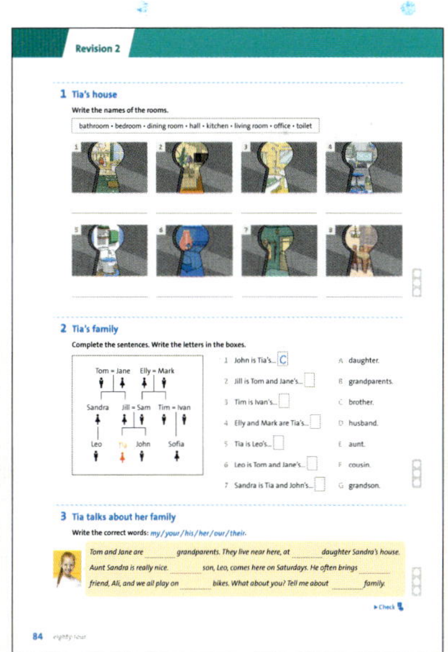

***Wordpower***

Auf dieser Seite findest du Übungen zu den Vokabeln der jeweiligen Units und kannst dein gesprochenes Englisch verbessern.

***My learner log***

Hier kannst du auf die Unit zurückblicken und deinen Lernstand festhalten.

***Revision***

Halte auf diesen Seiten inne und wiederhole, was du in den vorherigen Units gelernt hast.

## Diese Verweise führen dich in die *Diff bank* am Ende der Unit

▶ More help

Hilfen zu den Aufgaben

▶ Early finisher

weitere Übungen

▶ Challenge

weitere Übungen mit höherem Schwierigkeitsgrad

## Dein Buch findest du auch in der Cornelsen Lernen App

Siehst du eines dieser Symbole in deinem Workbook, kannst du in deiner App …

alle Hörtexte und Videos zu deinem Buch aufrufen.

auf Ideen und Hilfen zugreifen.

▶ Check

deine Antworten eigenständig überprüfen.

# lighthouse 1

Workbook Lehrkräftefassung

*Im Auftrag des Verlages erarbeitet von*
Gwen Berwick, York
Sydney Thorne, York

*In Zusammenarbeit mit der Englischredaktion*
Klaus Unger (Projektleitung),
Franziska Gräbe (verantwortliche Redakteurin), Lisa Ahmadi, Doreen Arnold, Natalie-Monique Bernau, Bernd Freiling, Cornelia Frisse, Mara Leibowitz, Christine Maxwell, Jutta Seuren, Kathrin Spiegelberg, Karin Wedepohl, Silvia Wiedemann, Olivia Wintgens, Anja Zieschang

*Beratende Mitwirkung*
Anke Barth, Plauen; Armin Düpmeier, Warendorf; Lara Jano, Rottweil

*Lizenzmanagement*
Silke Kirchhoff

*Illustrationen*
Harald Ardeias, Schelkingen; Irina Zinner, Hamburg

*Fotos*
Anja Poehlmann, Brighton
Für die freundliche Unterstützung danken wir der *Varndean School, Brighton*

*Umschlaggestaltung*
Rosendahl, Berlin

*Layoutkonzept*
Klein & Halm, Berlin

*Layout und technische Umsetzung*
Reemers Publishing Services GmbH

*Druck*
Parzeller print & media GmbH & Co. KG, Fulda

ISBN 978-3-0603-6253-0
ISBN 978-3-0603-4544-1 Lehrkräftefassung

PEFC zertifiziert
Dieses Produkt stammt aus nachhaltig bewirtschafteten Wäldern und kontrollierten Quellen.
www.pefc.de
PEFC/04-31-1308

**www.cornelsen.de**



1. Auflage, 1. Druck 2022

Alle Drucke dieser Auflage sind inhaltlich unverändert und können im Unterricht nebeneinander verwendet werden.



Passend zum Workbook:
Sprechen, Aussprache, Wortschatz und Grammatik digital üben mit der mobilen App ChatClass. Erhältlich auch als PrintPlus-Klassenlizenz bei Nutzung des Arbeitsheftes.

# lighthouse 1

## Workbook Lehrkräftefassung

**Audios** online verfügbar unter
www.cornelsen.de/webcodes **Code:** tavebo

Dein Workbook findest du auch in der Cornelsen Lernen App.

Siehst du eines dieser Symbole in deinem Workbook, findest du in der App …

 alle **Audios**

 alle **Videos** und **Erklärfilme**

 **Hilfen** und **Lösungen** zu ausgewählten Aufgaben

Cornelsen

**Titelbild**
Cornelsen/Personen: Anja Poehlmann, Brighton Pier: mauritius images/Steve Vidler

**Illustrationen**
Cornelsen/**Harald Ardeias**: (S. 8, S. 10 1-7, S.13 Safari Park, S. 14, S. 15 unten S. 16, S. 17, S. 19 oben, S. 24 1-9, S. 25, S. 27 unten re., S. 28, S. 30, S. 32, S. 33, S. 35, S. 38, S. 41, S. 44, S. 46 A-H, S. 49 mitte re. S. 51 außer Herzen, S. 53, S. 55, S. 59, S. 60 oben, S. 64, S. 73, S. 76, S. 81, S. 84). Cornelsen/**Irina Zinner**: (S. 5 Möwe, S. 6 Möwe, S. 7 Möwe, S. 13 Möwe, S. 22 Möwe, S. 23 Möwe, S. 27 Möwe, S. 29 Möwe, S. 39 Möwe, S. 41 Möwe, S, 42 Möwe, S. 50 Möwe, S. 56 Möwe, S. 59 Möwe, S. 59 Möwe, S. 66 Möwe, S. 77 Möwe, S. 79 Möwe, S. 80 Möwe, S. 88 Möwen). **Ungermeyer**: (S. 6+7 Krallenabdrücke); **Miniaturseiten Umschlag**: Siehe jeweilige Seite.

**Abbildungen**
**Miniaturseiten Umschlag**: Siehe jeweilige Seite; **S. 5:** Cornelsen/Anja Poehlmann; **S. 6+7** Hintergrund: Shutterstock.com/vetryanaya_o; **S. 9** 1: Shutterstock.com/Utekhina Anna, 2: Shutterstock.com/Four Oaks, 3: Shutterstock.com/PHOTOCREO Michal Bednarek, 4: Shutterstock.com/Eric Isselee, 5: Shutterstock.com/bluedog studio, 6: stock.adobe.com/Arija, 7: Shutterstock.com/SmileKorn, 8: Shutterstock.com/Eric Isselee, Emoticons: stock.adobe.com/streptococcus; **S. 10** unten li.: stock.adobe.com/markus_marb, unten re.: Cornelsen/Oliver Meibert; **S. 11** oben: stock.adobe.com/sepy, mitte li.: stock.adobe.com/Janina_PLD, mitte re.: stock.adobe.com/anamejia18, Flaggen: stock.adobe.com/Porcupen; **S. 12** A: ClipDealer GmbH/SeanPrior, B: stock.adobe.com/pololia, C: stock.adobe.com/Jacek Chabraszewski, D: stock.adobe.com/DragonImages, E: stock.adobe.com/Alena Yakusheva, F: ClipDealer GmbH/Wavebreak Media LTD, G: mauritius images/alamy stock photo/Ian Allenden, H: stock.adobe.com/JackF, unten mi.: Cornelsen/Anja Poehlmann; **S. 15** oben re.: stock.adobe.com/Syda Productions/lev dolgachov; **S. 18** A: stock.adobe.com/.shock, B: Shutterstock.com/Monkey Business Images, C: stock.adobe.com/vladimirnenezic, D: mauritius images/Johnér, E: stock.adobe.com/smolaw11, F: stock.adobe.com/Gudellaphoto; **S. 19** 1: Shutterstock.com/Only_NewPhoto, 2: stock.adobe.com/Imcsike, 3: stock.adobe.com/Fabio Principe, 4: Shutterstock.com/Syda Productions, 5: stock.adobe.com/SB Arts Media, 6: stock.adobe.com/Photographee.eu/Katarzyna Bialasiewicz, 7: stock.adobe.com/Tyler Olson, 8: stock.adobe.com/Africa Studio; **S. 21** unten re.: Cornelsen/Oliver Meibert, **S. 23** unten mi.: Cornelsen/Anja Poehlmann; **S. 24** A: stock.adobe.com/.shock, B: Shutterstock.com/Monkey Business Images, C: stock.adobe.com/vladimirnenezic, D: mauritius images/Johnér, E: stock.adobe.com/smolaw11, F: stock.adobe.com/Gudellaphoto; **S. 25**: Shutterstock.com/Rvector; **S. 26** Oscar: stock.adobe.com/Peredniankina, Dad's Mum: Shutterstock.com/PHILIPIMAGE, My Mum: stock.adobe.com/francescoridolfi.com/Rido, Mum's Mum: Shutterstock.com/Caftor, Amelia: Shutterstock.com/Olga Sapegina, Freddie: Shutterstock.com/Max Topchii, Dad's Dad: Shutterstock.com/Alejandro Camacho B, Mike: stock.adobe.com/goodluz, Olivia: Shutterstock.com/Erika Cross, Jane: stock.adobe.com/#CNF, My Dad: Shutterstock.com/Joshua Rainey Photography; **S. 27** Fische: Shutterstock.com/panpilai paipa, Papageien: Shutterstock.com/Super Prin, Hasen: Shutterstock.com/Kolomiyets Viktoriya, Katzen: Shutterstock.com/Peti74, Pferde: Shutterstock.com/Kwadrat, Schlangen: Shutterstock.com/Mufti Adi Utomo, Hunde: Shutterstock.com/thka, Hamster: mauritius images/alamy stock photo/Maximilian Weinzierl; **S. 29** 1: Shutterstock.com/BearFotos, 2: Shutterstock.com/anggitirta, 3: Shutterstock.com/Felipe Cespedes G, 4: Shutterstock.com/Alex Milan; **S. 31** 1: Imago Stock & People GmbH/Shotshop, 2: Shutterstock.com/Evgeny Karandaev, 3: Shutterstock.com/Africa Studio, 4: Shutterstock.com/donatas1205, 5: Shutterstock.com/Sachiczko, 6: Shutterstock.com/Mile Atanasov, 7: Shutterstock.com/YK; **S. 40** oben li. (Oscar): stock.adobe.com/Peredniankina, A: mauritius images/alamy stock photo/Katy Blackwood, B: stock.adobe.com/VaLiza/valiza14, C: mauritius images/alamy stock photo/John Michaels, D: Shutterstock.com/Kryvenok Anastasiia, E: stock.adobe.com/Suriyo; **S. 42**: Cornelsen/Oliver Meibert, **S. 43**: Shutterstock.com/ANURAK PONGPATIMET; **S. 45**: Shutterstock.com/Varlamova Lydmila; **S. 47**: Cornelsen/Oliver Meibert; **S. 48**: Cornelsen/Grasshopper Films (Filmstill); **S. 49** Zane: Cornelsen/Anja Poehlmann, Dad: Shutterstock.com/Daniel M Ernst; **S. 51** oben re.: stock.adobe.com/markus_marb, Herzen: Shutterstock.com/pking4th; **S. 52**: Shutterstock.com/ANURAK PONGPATIMET; **S. 54**: Shutterstock.com/Volodymyr Krasyuk; **S. 56** A: Imago Stock & People GmbH/Loop Images/Chris Harris, B: Imago Stock & People GmbH/Tim Oram, C: Imago Stock & People GmbH/Design Pics/Dosfotos, D: stock.adobe.com/Kevin Eaves, E: Imago Stock & People GmbH/robertharding/Baxter Bradford, F: stock.adobe.com/Nomad_Soul, G: stock.adobe.com/lev dolgachov/Syda Productions, H: Imago Stock & People GmbH/robertharding/Frank Fell, unten re.: mauritius images/alamy stock photo/keith morris, **S. 57**: Cornelsen/Anja Poehlmann; **S. 58** oben li.: stock.adobe.com/Porcupen, oben re.: stock.adobe.com/Porcupen, unten re.: Cornelsen/Anja Poehlmann; **S. 60** Chandra: mauritius images/Westend61, Oscar: stock.adobe.com/Peredniankina; **S. 61** oben li.: Imago Stock & People GmbH/robertharding/Stuart Black, unten li.: Imago Stock & People GmbH/robertharding/Jeanne Rawlings, England: stock.adobe.com/cyclingscot; **S. 62** oben li.: stock.adobe.com/lesniewski, mitte re.: mauritius images/alamy stock photo/Howard Taylor, Wetter: Shutterstock.com/Zelimir Zarkovic; **S. 63** oben li.: mauritius images/alamy stock photo/Jason Chillmaid, oben re.: mauritius images/alamy stock photo/Hoi Tung Wong, Flyer: Shutterstock.com/Greenni; **S. 70** A: Shutterstock.com/Alexander Raths, B: Shutterstock.com/azure1, C: Shutterstock.com/bigacis, D: Shutterstock.com/cigdem, E: Shutterstock.com/nortongo, F: Shutterstock.com/Valery121283, G: Shutterstock.com/Alexander Raths, H: Shutterstock.com/morgenstjerne, I: Shutterstock.com/Tim UR, J: Shutterstock.com/MaraZe; **S. 71** A: stock.adobe.com/karelnoppe, B: Shutterstock.com/aldegonde, C: Shutterstock.com/Ixepop, D: Shutterstock.com/Apollofoto, E: Shutterstock.com/RedPanda21, F: stock.adobe.com/patramansky; **S. 72** 1: Shutterstock.com/Vitalinka, 2: Shutterstock.com/aarrows, 3+4: Shutterstock.com/Eladora, 5: Shutterstock.com/shaineast, 6: Shutterstock.com/majivecka; **S. 74** A: Shutterstock.com/Marietjie, B: stock.adobe.com/Serge Aubert, C: stock.adobe.com/Margarita, D: stock.adobe.com/hartphotography; **S. 75** 1: Shutterstock.com/Svetlana Serebryakova, 2: Shutterstock.com/Pawel_Brzozowski, 3: stock.adobe.com/tpzijl, 4: stock.adobe.com/rdnzl, 5: stock.adobe.com/DenisNata; **S. 76** 1: Shutterstock.com/Perutskyi Petro, 2: Shutterstock.com/bigacis, 3: Shutterstock.com/karen roach, 4: Shutterstock.com/Andrii Horulko, 5: Shutterstock.com/Angel Simon, 6: Shutterstock.com/Ruslan Ivantsov; **S. 77** oben li.: Shutterstock.com/sirtravelalot; **S. 78**: Cornelsen/Grasshopper Films (Filmstill); **S. 82** 1: Shutterstock.com/Vitalinka, 2: Shutterstock.com/aarrows, 3+4: Shutterstock.com/Eladora, 5: Shutterstock.com/shaineast, 6: Shutterstock.com/majivecka; **S. 84** unten li.: Shutterstock.com/ViDI Studio, Figuren: stock.adobe.com; **S. 86** oben li.: Imago Stock & People GmbH/robertharding/Jeanne Rawlings, unten li.: Imago Stock & People GmbH/robertharding/Stuart Black, England: stock.adobe.com/cyclingscot; **S. 87** 1: stock.adobe.com/karandaev, 2: Shutterstock.com/Nativania, 3: stock.adobe.com/ExQuisine, 4: stock.adobe.com/svetamart, 5: Shutterstock.com/ivanoffotography

| | |
|---|---|
| So lernst du mit Lighthouse | U2 |
| Impressum | 2 |
| Quellenverzeichnis | 4 |
| Inhaltsverzeichnis | 5 |
| **My English book** | 6 |
| **Hello!** **Nice to meet you** | 8 |
| Unit 1 **My new school** | 12 |
| Unit 2 **My family and home** | 26 |
| Unit 3 **My day** | 40 |
| **Revision 1** | 54 |
| Unit 4 **Where I live** | 56 |
| Unit 5 **Enjoy!** | 70 |
| **Revision 2** | 84 |
| **Partner pages** | 86 |
| Typical tasks | 88 |

## This quiz helps you get to know your *Lighthouse* student's book.

**Mit diesem Quiz lernst du dein *Lighthouse*-Schulbuch kennen.**
**Du kannst es allein oder mit einem Partner / einer Partnerin lösen.**

1 Wieviele Units hat dein *Lighthouse*-Schulbuch?  5

2 Jede Unit beginnt mit einer Übersicht darüber, was du darin lernen wirst: *Nach dieser Unit kann ich ...*

In welcher Unit lernst du, über deine Family und Haustiere zu sprechen?

Unit 2

3 In Unit 1 lernst du die Lehrwerkskinder kennen. Nenne ihre Namen.

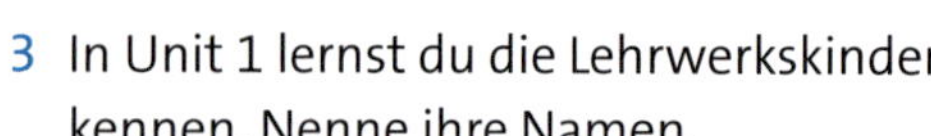

Sunita, Noah, Zane, Lily

4 Was bedeutet dieses Symbol? ⊠ Schaue am Anfang des Schulbuchs auf den *So lernst du mit Lighthouse-Seiten* nach.

schwierige Aufgabe

5 In der *Cornelsen Lernen App* findest du viele nützliche Dinge. Welches Symbol im Buch weist auf digitale Hilfen hin?

6 Auf vielen Seiten findest du unten das  Digital quiz -Symbol. Was kannst du hier tun?

zu jedem Unitteil ein Quiz in der App machen

7 Was bedeuten diese 4 Begriffe in der *Diff bank*? Ordne die Buchstaben zu.

 C  More practice  B More help

 D Challenge  A Parallel exercise

A einfachere Variante einer Übung
B Hilfen zu den Aufgaben
C weitere Übungen
D weitere Übungen mit höherem Schwierigkeitsgrad

8 Es gibt kleinere Lernaufgaben am Ende jedes Topics und größere am Ende jeder Unit.

Sie heißen: My task und Unit task.

16 Finde die *Let's talk*-Seiten. Wozu dienen die Redewendungen unter Punkt 7?

Feedback geben

9 Wie heißen die letzten 4 grünen Seiten jeder Unit, auf denen du dein Wissen überprüfen kannst?

Checkpoint

15 Wo kannst du nachschauen, wenn du eine Arbeitsanweisung nicht verstehst?

☐ S. 213 ☐ S. 254 ☑ S. 284

10 Du möchtest eine Grammatikregel nachschauen, zum Beispiel wie man im Englischen den Plural bildet. Wo kannst du nachschlagen?

☐ Skills file ☑ Language file

☐ Wordbanks

14 Was heißt *seagull* auf Deutsch?

Möwe

Und wo findest du diese Information?

Im Dictionary auf Seite 263.

11 Schaue in das *Skills file* und nenne 3 Methoden, die dort erklärt sind.

Wörter lernen, Mindmaps, Buchstabieren

13 Im *Vocabulary* findest du die neuen Wörter aus jeder Unit. Lies den Eintrag zu *chocolate* auf S. 231. Worauf musst du achten?

auf die Betonung

12 Finde die Karte der Britischen Inseln. Wie heißt die Nordsee auf Englisch?

The North Sea

**Prima! Nun weißt du schon viel über dein *Lighthouse*-Schulbuch. Du kannst deine Lösungen in der App überprüfen.** Check

# Hello!
# Nice to meet you

## 1 Hello

▸ SB, p. 13

**Look at the picture. Write the words.**

about • fine • how • hungry • like • ~~name~~ • nice • see • so • too • where • years

I can say hello.

## 2 Animals

► SB, p. 14

a) Find the animals: → ↓ ↘. Write the correct words.

| E | J | P | I | X | R | A | D |
|---|---|---|---|---|---|---|---|
| N | L | I | O | N | U | P | V |
| H | R | E | T | M | H | N | D |
| Q | P | G | P | J | S | D | O |
| C | A | T | F | H | N | M | G |
| O | R | M | I | D | A | B | M |
| M | R | D | O | K | K | N | I |
| F | O | B | C | N | E | L | T |
| X | T | D | A | G | K | Y | Q |
| T | A | H | O | R | S | E | G |
| J | B | I | W | R | A | G | Y |

1 
d o g

2 e l e p h a n t

3 
c a t

4 m o n k e y

5 
s n a k e

6 
h o r s e

7 
p a r r o t

8 l i o n

b) Complete the sentence.

My favourite animal is ______________________

## 3 Hobbies

► SB, p. 15

a) Look at the pictures and sentences. Right (✓) or wrong (✗)?

✓ / ✗

1  – *I love listening to music.* ✗

2   – *I like drawing.* ✓

3  – *I don't like dancing.* ✓

4  – *I like taking photos.* ✗

5  – *I don't like swimming.* ✗

6  – *I love football.* ✓

b) Write two sentences about you. *(I love… / I like… / I don't like…)*

______________________

I can talk about what I like. ✓

## 4 Oscar's things

▶ SB, p. 15

Look at the pictures. Write what Oscar says.

| | | |
|---|---|---|
| cap | | black |
| bag | big | blue |
| guitar | small | gold |
| bike | new | green |
| chain | old | purple |
| scooter | | silver |
| mobile phone | | yellow |

1 

2 

3 

4 

5 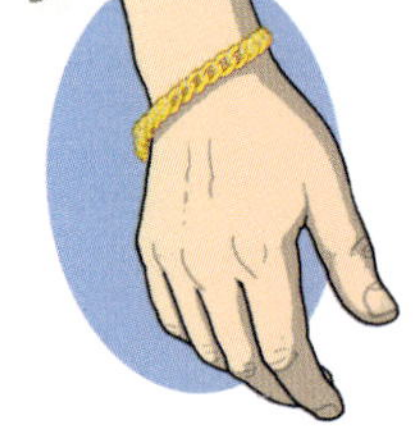

6 7 

1 *My cap is old and green.*
2 *My bag is big and purple.*
3 *My guitar is old and blue.*
4 *My bike is new and silver.*
5 *My chain is small and gold.*
6 *My scooter is old and yellow.*
7 *My mobile phone is new and black.*

## 5 Talk, talk, talk!

SB, p. 16

01 a) LISTENING Listen to Jasmine and Max. Tick (✓) what they talk about.

- How are you? ☐
- What's your name? ☑
- Where are you from? ☑
- How old are you? ☑
- I like ... what about you? ☑
- favourite sport ☑
- favourite colour ☐
- favourite hobby ☑
- favourite animal ☐
- favourite thing ☑

b) SPEAKING Talk, talk, talk with your partner. How many minutes / seconds[1] can you talk? ▶ Digital help

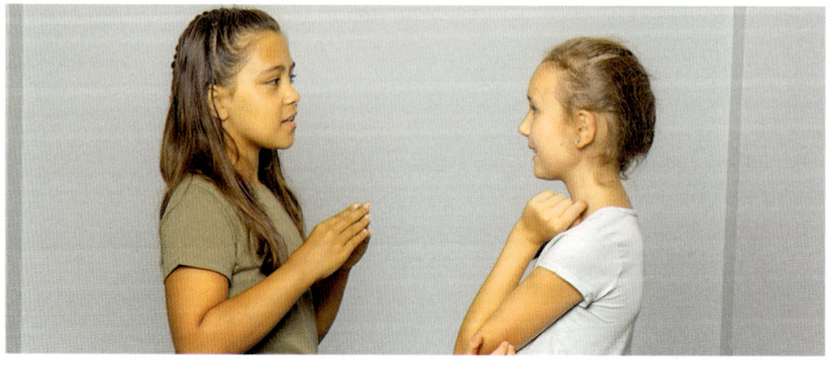

[1] how many minutes / seconds *wie viele Minuten / Sekunden*

## 6 In class

▸ SB, p. 17

a) Write the correct words.

books • close • down • hand • look • please • quiet • up

1 *Stand* up.

2 *Open your* books.

3 *Put your* hand *up.*

4 *Listen* please.

5 *Sit* down.

6 Quiet, *please*

7 Close *your books.*

8 Look *at me.*

b) Mime an instruction[1]. Your partner says it.

Partner A – 4 instructions
Partner B – 4 instructions

*Quiet, please.*

*Yes, right!*

## 7 In your book

▸ SB, p. 17

Match the English words and the German words.

| | | | | |
|---|---|---|---|---|
| 1 | **Find** Scout. | D | A | Schreibe die richtigen Wörter. |
| 2 | **Complete** the song. | B | B | Vervollständige das Lied. |
| 3 | Listen and **repeat**. | E | C | Ordne die Wörter den Bildern zu. |
| 4 | **Write** the correct **words**. | A | D | Finde Scout. |
| 5 | **Right** or **wrong**? | F | E | Höre zu und wiederhole. |
| 6 | **Match** the words and the **pictures**. | C | F | Richtig oder falsch? |

[1] **instruction** *Anweisung*

I can understand classroom English.

# Unit 1
# My new school

## 1 Sports and hobbies

▶ SB, p. 19

Write the eight words.

A 
B 
C 
D 

reading — cooking — walking — coding

E 
F 
G 
H 

parkour — yoga — badminton — dancing

## 2 Zane and you

▶ Digital help ▶ SB, p. 19

a) Write the missing words.

are • favourite • like • where • your

1 Hi. I'm Zane. What's *your* name?

2 How old *are* you?

3 I'm from Brighton.

*Where* are you from?

4 I *like* cooking and dancing.

What about you?

5 My *favourite* sport is swimming.

What about you?

b) Write your answers.

1 *Hi. I'm ...*

2 *I'm 11 / 12 (years old).*

3 *I'm from ...*

4 *I like ...*

5 *My favourite sport is ...*

I can understand students at a British school.

## 3 Lily, Zane, Sunita and Noah

▶ Digital help ▶ SB, p. 20

Find the words. Then complete the sentences.

| | | |
|---|---|---|
| 1 | firneds | Zane and Lily are *friends*. |
| 2 | tride | Zane is busy and *tired*. |
| 3 | hyapp | Lily is *happy* about the school tie. |
| 4 | sacerd | Noah is *scared* of the school. |
| 5 | ufimorn | Sunita and Noah like the *uniform*. |
| 6 | smae | Sunita and Noah are in the *same* class. |

## 4 Language *a/an* In a safari park

▶ SB, p. 21

Look at the pictures. Then complete the sentences.
Write *a* or *an*.

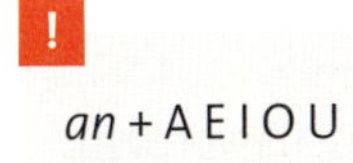

I can see (1) *an* animal. It's (2) *a* big animal. It's (3) *an* elephant. That's cool!

I can see (4) *an* animal too! (5) *A* small animal. It's (6) *a* snake. (7) *An* orange snake. It's horrible!

And I can see (8) *a* dog. (9) *A* small dog. (10) *An* English dog. And I love it!

## 5 School things

▶ More help, p. 24 ▶ SB, p. 21

**a) Look at the pictures. Write the words.**

1 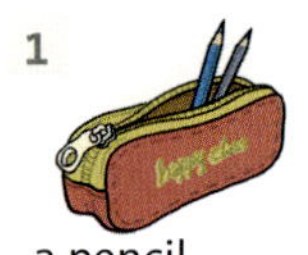
a pencil ...

2 
a pencil ...

3 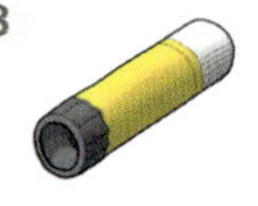
a ... stick

4 

5 

6 
an exercise ...

7 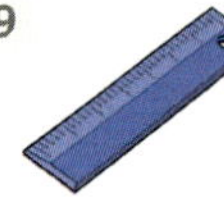

8

9

|  |  |  |  |  |  | 2 |  |  |
|---|---|---|---|---|---|---|---|---|
|  |  | 3 | 1 | C | A | S | E |  |
|  |  | G |  |  |  | H |  | 4 |
|  |  | L |  | 6 |  | A |  | P |
| 5 | R | U | B | B | E | R |  | E |
|  |  | E |  | O | 7 | P | E | N |
|  |  |  |  | O |  | E |  | C |
| 8 | D | E | S | K |  | N |  | I |
|  |  |  |  |  |  | E |  | L |
|  | 9 | R | U | L | E | R |  |  |

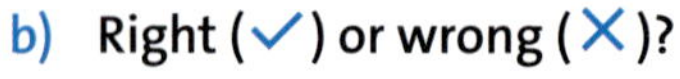

**b) Right (✓) or wrong (✗)?**

1 The ruler is purple. ✓

2 The pencil is brown. ✗

3 The rubber is an elephant! ✓

4 The pencil case is green and black. ✗

5 The pencil sharpener is a dog! ✗

6 The pen is blue and white. ✓

## 6 What can you see?

▶ SB, p. 22

**Look at the picture. Complete the sentence.**

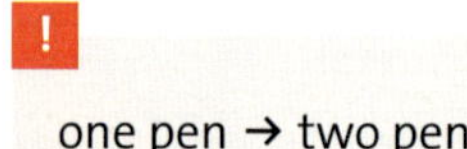
!
one pen → two pens

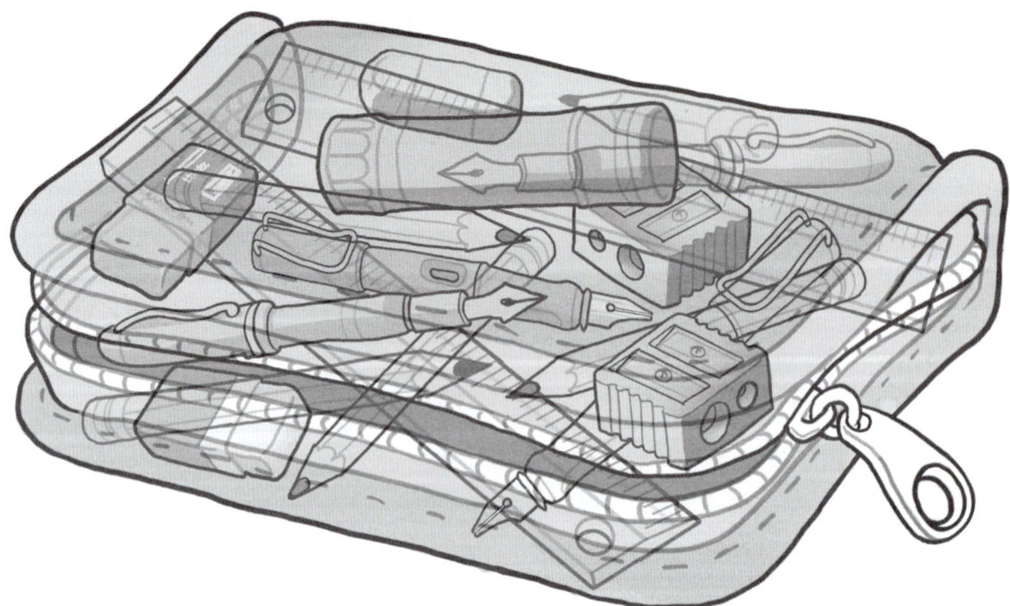

In the pencil case there are... two pencil sharpeners, one glue stick, three rubbers, two rulers, four pens, five pencils.

▶ Challenge 1, p. 25

## 7 Questions in an English lesson class

▶ Digital help ▶ SB, p. 23

**Write the words in the right order.**

1 I / use / pencil / please / can / your / ?
*Can I use your pencil, please?*

2 window / open / can / the / I / please / ?
*Can I open the window, please?*

3 what's / answer / question / the / to / five / ?
*What's the answer to question five?*

4 can / you / again / that / say / ?
*Can you say that again?*

5 you / can / me / understand / ?
*Can you understand me?*

6 I/ toilet / the / go / can / to / ?
*Can I go to the toilet?*

7 question two / help / can / me / with / you / ?
*Can you help me with question two?*

## 8 We're all new in this school!

▶ SB, p. 24

**Write the correct words from the box.**

I • you • he • she • we • you • they

I can understand and use classroom English.

## 9 Language *to be* It's break at Varndean School

Erklärfilm

▶ SB, p. 24

Write the correct words from the box.

I'm • you're • he's • it's • she's • they're • we're

## 10 Days of the week

▶ SB, p. 25

a) Highlight the six days of the week.

b) Write the missing day: Saturday

## 11 LISTENING A different school: Pelham School

▸ SB, p. 26

02

**Listen to five lessons. Write 1–5 next to the subjects.**

| | | | | |
|---|---|---|---|---|
| English ☐ | maths 1 | art ☐ | French 5 | geography 2 |
| history ☐ | music 3 | PE 4 | science ☐ | computing ☐ |

## 12 The timetable in Pelham School

▸ SB, p. 27

03

**a)** LISTENING **Listen to Daniel. What are Daniel's two favourite subjects?**

history and PE

03

**b)** LISTENING **Look at the timetable and listen again. Is Daniel's information right (✓) or wrong (✗)?**

Monday ✗ Tuesday ✗ Wednesday ✓ Thursday ✗ Friday ✓

| Monday | Tuesday | Wednesday | Thursday | Friday |
|---|---|---|---|---|
| | | | | |
| | | | | |
| break | break | break | break | break |
| | | | | |
| lunch | lunch | lunch | lunch | lunch |
| | | | | |

**c)** SPEAKING **Look again at the timetable.**
**Talk to a partner. Use different subjects and different days.**

Partner A: *Maths is ...*
*... on Monday, Wednesday and Friday.* :Partner B

Partner B: *After lunch on Wednesday it's ...*
*... music.* :Partner A

**I can write my timetable in English.** ✓

## 13 What about you?

▶ SB, p. 27

**What do you like? What don't you like? Write five sentences.**

| | | | | |
|---|---|---|---|---|
| I like<br>I don't like | elephants<br>science<br>badminton<br>my friends<br>school uniforms<br>holidays<br>swimming | because | it's<br>they're | horrible.<br>clever.<br>hard.<br>cool.<br>nice.<br>big. |

1 *(I like holidays because they're cool.)*

2 *(I don't like badminton because it's hard.)*

3 *(I like swimming because it's cool.)*

4 *(I don't like school uniforms because they're horrible.)*

5 *(I like my friends because they're nice.)*

## 14 Places in school

▶ Digital help ▶ More help, p. 24 ▶ SB, p. 28

**Show a friend the places in school. Write the missing words.**

A

This is the sports *h a l l*.

B

This is the *a r t* room.

C

History and music are in this *b u i l d i n g*.

D

This is the *c a n t e e n*. We have lunch here.

E

This is the big *c o r r i d o r*.

F

And this is my *f a v o u r i t e* place because I love *s w i m m i n g*!

## 15 LANGUAGE *to be* (negative) Lunchtime at Varndean School

Erklär-film

► SB, p. 29

**Fill the gaps with the right words: *aren't / isn't / 'm not.***

## 16 LANGUAGE *to be* (positive and negative)

► SB, p. 29

**Write the right form of *to be*.**

1 This isn't a pencil case.

5 I'm scared.

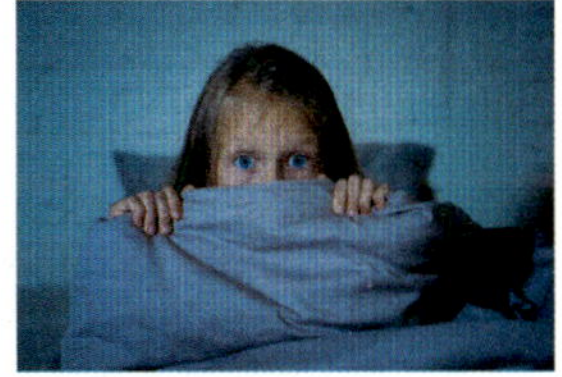

2 We are tired!

6 The students are in the sports hall.

3 We aren't happy.

7 He's asleep.

4 I'm not in Brighton.

8 She isn't lucky!

I can describe my school.

## 17 READING People in the story

▶ SB, pp. 30–32

**Look at the story on pages 30–32 in your book. Write the name or names.**

Jade • Kyle • Lily • Noah • Noah's dad • Scout and friends • Sunita • Zane

1 He's maybe the star in a band. *Zane*
2 They're bullies. *Kyle, Jade*
3 He's in trouble. *Noah*
4 She's scared of Kyle and Jade at first. *Lily*
5 They're helpful. *Scout and friends*
6 They're brave. *Lily, Sunita*
7 He's good with animals. *Noah*
8 He's happy to meet Noah's friends. *Noah's dad*

## 18 READING The right endings

▶ SB, pp. 30–32

**Match 1–6 to the endings A–F. Draw lines.**

1 Zane isn't free after school because ...
2 Sunita likes Zane because ...
3 Lily and Sunita are sad because ...
4 Scout is horrible to Kyle and Jade because ...
5 Lily and Sunita are brave because ...
6 Lily and Sunita like Lucky because ...

A she says he's cool.
B Noah is in trouble.
C they help their friend Noah.
D he's really friendly.
E he's in a band.
F they are very mean to Noah.

## 19 READING Language in the story

▶ SB, pp. 30–32

**Write the right endings.**

are really mean. • for band now. • help him. • me. • of you. • to the beach.

1 Let's go *to the beach.*
2 It's time *for band now.*
3 Those bullies *are really mean.*
4 You understand *me.*
5 Let's *help him.*
6 We're not scared *of you.*

▶ Early finisher 1, 2, p. 23

I can understand a story about friends. 

## 20 Wrong word

**Which word is wrong? Why? Use words from the box.**

animal • character word • colour • hobby • number • place • sport • subject

1 two eight Wednesday fifteen — *Wednesday* is wrong because it isn't a *number*.
2 lion dog ruler snake — *ruler* because it isn't an *animal*.
3 map grey blue white — *map* because it isn't a *colour*.
4 football badminton swimming reading — *reading* because it isn't a *sport*.
5 science French corridor history — *corridor* because it isn't a *subject*.
6 toilet classroom hall biology — *biology* because it isn't a *place*.
7 kind big mean brave — *big* because it isn't a *character word*.
8 drawing building reading cooking — *building* because it isn't a *hobby*.

## 21 Speaking Speak good English

04

**a) Listen to the words. Then listen again and repeat them.**

1 -i- as in six: stick British building minutes history
2 -i- as in five: like goodbye right design kind Hi!

**b) Write the words in the box in the right list.** ▸ Digital help

different • favourite • Friday • I'm • lion • mind map • my • pink • science • swim • this

| -i- as in six | -i- as in five |
|---|---|
| *different* | *Friday* |
| *favourite* | *I'm* |
| *pink* | *lion* |
| *swim* | *mind map* |
| *this* | *my* |
| | *science* |

05

**c) Now say these to your partner. Then listen and check your answers.**

1 We have design on Friday.
2 This is a different building.
3 Hi Lily! You're kind. Bye!
4 History is my favourite subject.
5 I'm right!
6 Mike is nice.
7 Swim for six minutes!
8 I like science.

**I think English is:**

fun ☐ hard ☐ OK ☐

**My favourite character:**

(Zane)

**Why:**

(He's cool. He's in a band.)

**My favourite phrases:**

Here you are!

(You're welcome!)

(I'm lucky!)

(I'm in trouble now!)

**My favourite words:**

seagull

(happy)

(horrible)

(food)

**Difficult words:**

friends

(design)

(science)

(because)

(building)

(weird)

**I remember:**

Lessons: art, (science, English, history, geography, PE, maths, computing, French, design and technology, biology)

Places in school: hall, (classroom, corridor, music room, canteen, sports hall)

Questions in class: Can I go to the toilet? (Can I open the window? Can I use your book? Can you say that again, please?)

Words to describe people: helpful, (busy, scared, nice, friendly, clever, mean)

**Learning English:**

Complete the smileys: ☺ = I like it. 😐 = It's OK. ☹ = I don't like it.

Speaking ◯ Listening ◯ Viewing ◯

Writing ◯ Story ◯ Learning words ◯

## Early finisher 1 A big game of small words

▸ Digital help

a) Read the sentence(s).
Circle the missing word, and write the red or blue letter here:

S E A G U L L S

Follow the arrow to the next box. Do the same again.

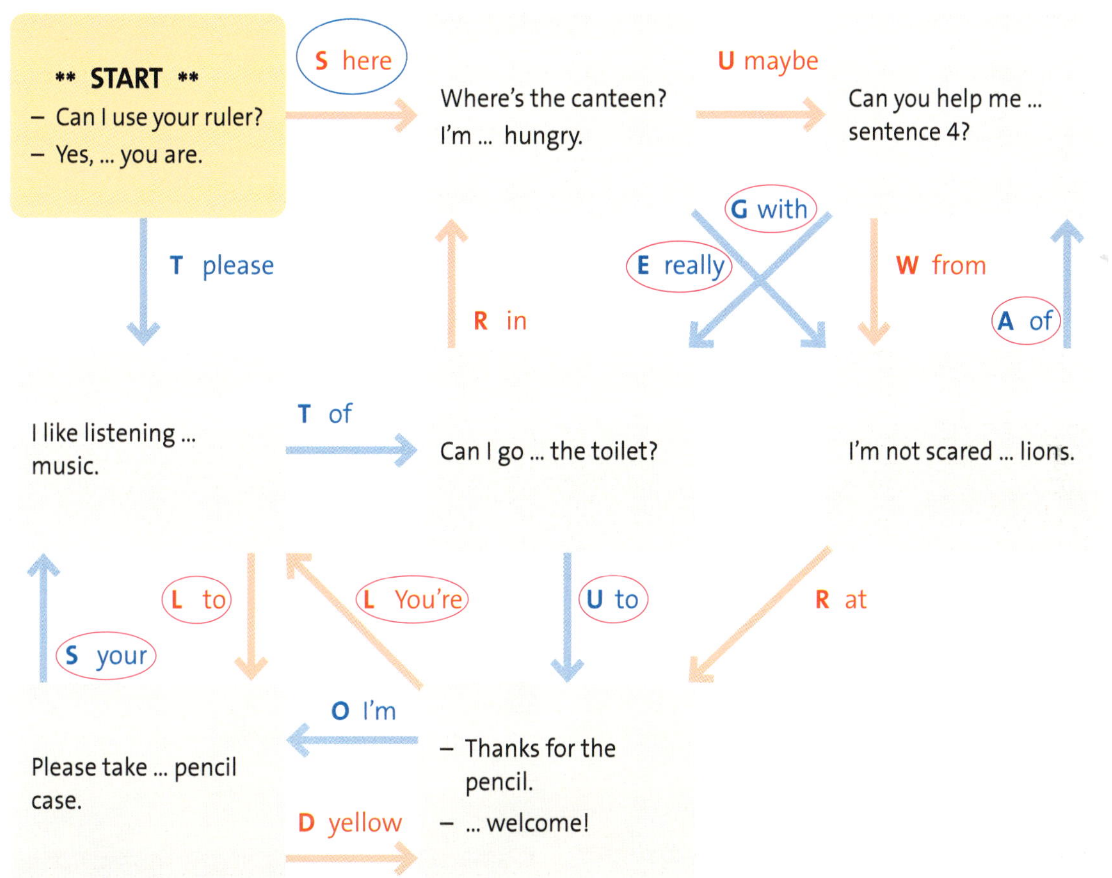


b) Now write a sentence with the word in a).

The s e a g u l l s are ... (horrible to Jade and Kyle.)

## Early finisher 2 WRITING As many sentences as you can

▸ Digital help

Write as many sentences as you can about Lily. Start all the sentences with *She's* ...

1 *She's Lily.*
2 *She's eleven.*
3 *She's ...*
4 *She's ...*
5 *She's at Varndean School.*
6 *She's ...*

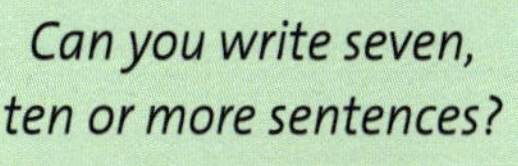

▸ Check

## More help 5 School things

▶ WB, p. 14 ▶ SB, p. 21

a) Look at the pictures. Write the words.

1 
a pencil ...

2 
a pencil ...

3 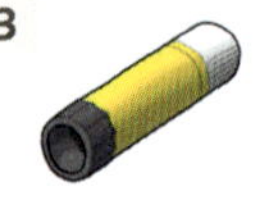
a ... stick

4 

5 

6 
an exercise ...

7 

8 

9

book • case • desk • glue • pen • pencil • rubber • ruler • sharpener

| | | | | | | 2 | | |
|---|---|---|---|---|---|---|---|---|
| | | 3 | 1 | C | A | S | E | |
| | | G | | | | H | | 4 |
| | | L | | 6 | | A | | P |
| 5 | R | U | B | B | E | R | | E |
| | | E | | O | 7 | P | E | N |
| | | | | O | | E | | C |
| 8 | D | E | S | K | | N | | I |
| | | | | | | E | | L |
| | 9 | R | U | L | E | R | | |

## More help 14 Places in school

▶ Digital help  ▶ WB, p. 18 ▶ SB, p. 28

Show a friend the places in school.
Write the missing words.

art • building • canteen • corridor • favourite • hall • swimming

A 

This is the sports h a l l.

B 

This is the a r t room.

C 

History and music are in this b u i l d i n g.

D 

This is the c a n t e e n. We have lunch here.

E 

This is the big c o r r i d o r.

F 

And this is my f a v o u r i t e place because I love s w i m m i n g!

## Challenge 1 A website for online shopping

▸ WB, p. 14

a) Look at the website. Are the things on the website for a) eating ☐ b) drinking ☐ or c) writing ☑ ?

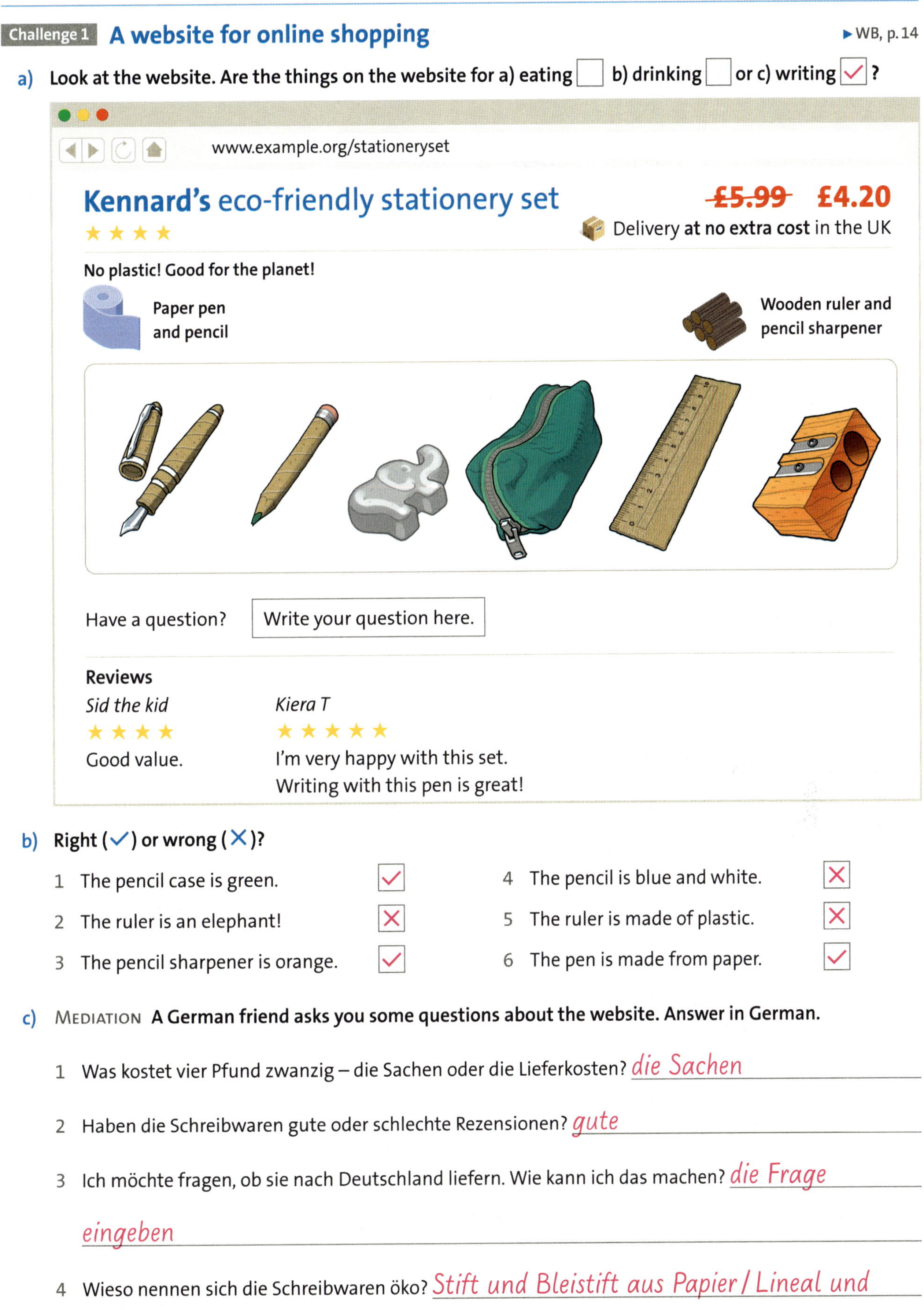


b) Right (✓) or wrong (✗)?

1 The pencil case is green. ☑
2 The ruler is an elephant! ☒
3 The pencil sharpener is orange. ☑
4 The pencil is blue and white. ☒
5 The ruler is made of plastic. ☒
6 The pen is made from paper. ☑

c) MEDIATION **A German friend asks you some questions about the website. Answer in German.**

1 Was kostet vier Pfund zwanzig – die Sachen oder die Lieferkosten? *die Sachen*

2 Haben die Schreibwaren gute oder schlechte Rezensionen? *gute*

3 Ich möchte fragen, ob sie nach Deutschland liefern. Wie kann ich das machen? *die Frage eingeben*

4 Wieso nennen sich die Schreibwaren öko? *Stift und Bleistift aus Papier / Lineal und Bleistiftspitzer aus Holz / kein Plastik*

▸ Check

# Unit 2
# My family and home

## 1 Oscar and his family

▸ SB, p. 49

a) Oscar is a student in 7C at Varndean School. Write Oscar's words about his family.

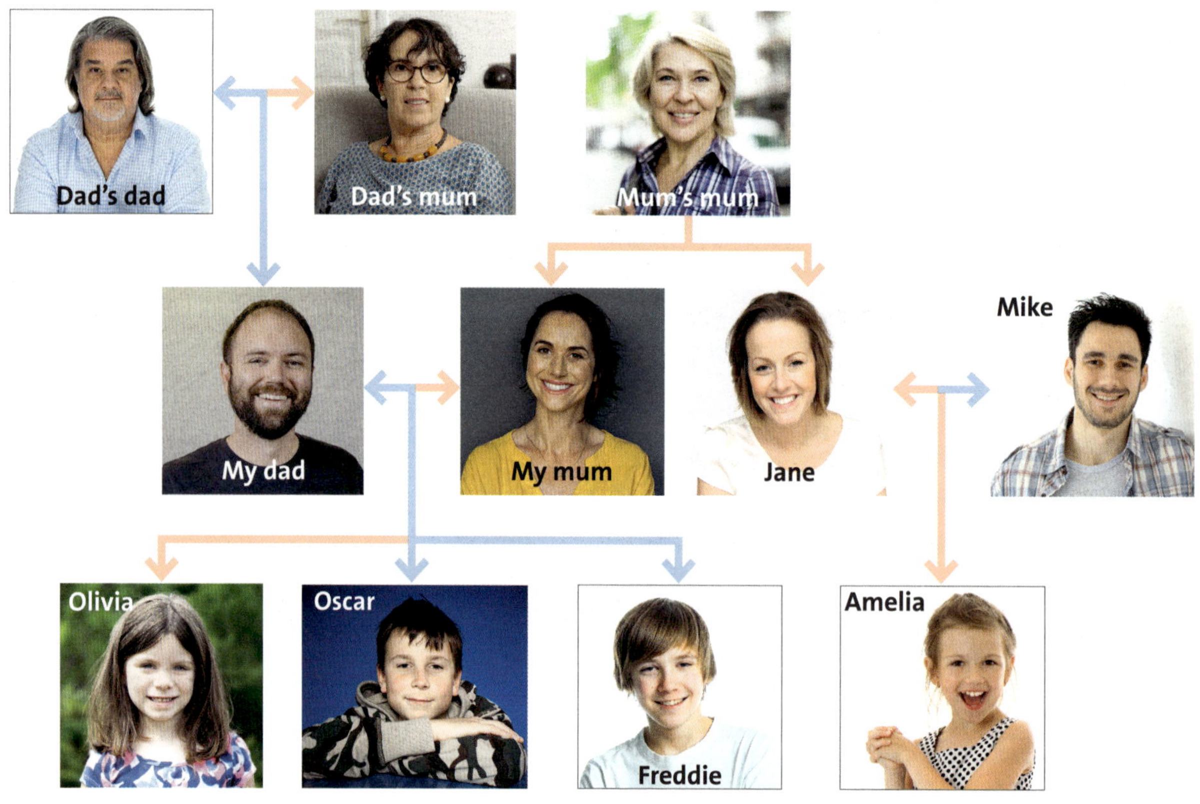


Hi, I'm Oscar. My sister is Olivia. Freddie is my brother. My mum's sister is my aunt Jane. She and my uncle Mike have one daughter, Amelia. Amelia is my cousin. I have two grandmas and one grandpa.

b) Look again at Oscar's family in a). Then complete the sentences with: *name + 's.*

1 Oscar's mum is Jane's sister.
2 Olivia is Oscar's sister.
3 Oscar is Freddie's brother.
4 Jane is Amelia's mum.
5 Amelia is Oscar's cousin.

I can talk about my family.

## 2 An animal puzzle

▶ SB, p. 50

**Look at the photos and read the sentences. Write the animal words in the plural.**

*One fish, two fish!*

1 Sssss! People are scared of us! We are *snakes*.

2 We are orange and blue. We can talk! We are *parrots*.

3 We swim and swim and swim. We are *fish*.

4 We hop – hop – hop! We are *rabbits*.

5 We are loud! But we are good friends of boys and girls. We are *dogs*.

6 We live in houses. We don't like swimming. Miaow! We are *cats*.

7 We are big. Some of us are white, some are brown, black or grey. We are *horses*.

8 We are small brown pets. We are *hamsters*.

## 3 George isn't happy!

▶ SB, p. 50

**a) Write the missing words.**

angry • have • house • I'm • It's • messy • of • quiet • Sunita's

1 *Hello,* I'm *George.* It's *the weekend and I'm not happy.*
2 *I live in* Sunita's *house.*
3 *I'm not happy because there are a lot* of *animals in the* house.
4 *We* have *a lot of animals because Meera is a vet.*
5 *I'm* angry *because the animals are loud, not* quiet.
6 *And I'm not happy because the house is* messy.

**b) Now check with your partner.**

Erklär-film

## 4 LANGUAGE Short answers All about you

► SB, p. 51

**Answer the questions. Use the answers in the box.**

Yes, I am. • Yes, we are. • No, I'm not. • No, we aren't.

1 Are you a girl? – Yes, I am. / No, I'm not.

2 Are you a boy? – Yes, I am. / No, I'm not.

3 Are you 11 years old? – Yes, I am. / No, I'm not.

4 Are you German? – Yes, I am. / No, I'm not.

5 Are you and your friends football fans? – Yes, we are. / No, we aren't.

6 Are you and your friends in Berlin? – Yes, we are. / No, we aren't.

## 5 LANGUAGE Questions and short answers Varndean School

► SB, p. 51

a) **Complete the questions with *is* or *are*.**

b) **Then check the information in Unit 1 of your book and write short answers with *yes* or *no*.**

1 Is Mr Lee a class teacher? – Yes, he is. ► p. 22

2 Is Mr Lee also a maths teacher? – No, he isn't. ► p. 22

3 Is Lily in 7F? – No, she isn't. ► p. 24

4 Are Sunita and Noah in 7C? – Yes, they are. ► p. 28

5 Is Zane in a band? – Yes, he is. ► p. 30

6 Are Kyle and Jade friends of Noah? – No, they aren't. ► p. 30

## 6 George, the parrot

► SB, p. 51

**George's sentences are wrong. Put in six apostrophes:** ' ' ' ' ' '

Hi, I'm George, Sunita's parrot.
We have a lot of animals from
Meera's work in the house. She's a vet.
Are the animals quiet? No, they aren't!
This isn't a good house for a parrot.

06

## 7 LISTENING Questions and answers about pets

► SB, p. 53

**a)** **Oscar asks his friends about their pets. Listen twice:**
**First listen and (circle) the right answer.**
**Then listen again and check your answers.**

*It's ok if you don't understand every word.*
*Read the sentences. Then listen for the information.*

1 Zara says dogs are too (loud) / difficult.

2 Oscar says Molly has an interesting name / (colour).

3 Noah says Daisy is very fast / (very old).

4 Ava says her hamster is (one year old) / two years old.

**b)** **Listen again and tick (✓) two boxes for each pet.**

1 Leo the lizard is ...

- A loud. ☐
- B quite friendly. ☑
- C very friendly. ☐
- D very active. ☑

2 Molly the cat is ...

- A mean. ☐
- B busy. ☑
- C quite small. ☑
- D very small. ☐

3 Daisy the dog is ...

- A small. ☐
- B quite slow. ☑
- C very slow. ☐
- D very special. ☑

4 Harry the hamster is ...

- A very friendly. ☑
- B messy. ☐
- C quiet. ☐
- D very interesting. ☑

I can talk about pets. ✓

## 8 Oscar's new flat

▶ SB, p. 55

**a) Write the missing words.**

We have the f l a t at the top with a nice b a l c o n y.

There are three big t r e e s in the g a r d e n.

We have nice n e i g h b o u r s on the ground floor.

**b) What's missing in the picture? Use the letters in the boxes and write the word.** A g a r a g e.

**c) Now look at the pictures of the rooms in Oscar's flat. Write the sentences.**

! *There's* + singular: There's a cat here.
*There are* + plural: There are two cats here.

1 There's a living room.

2 There are three bedrooms.

3 There's an office.

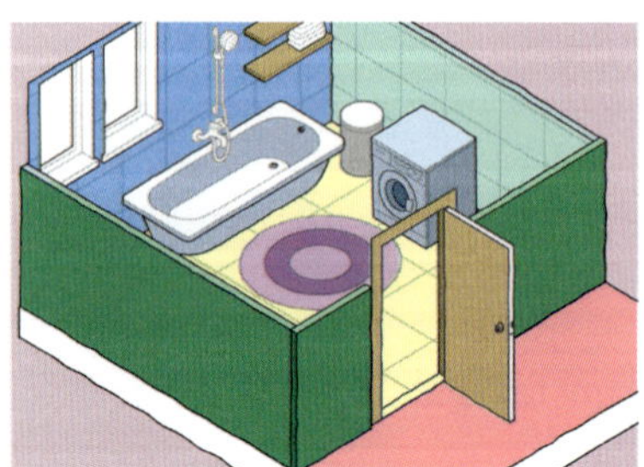

4 There's a bathroom.

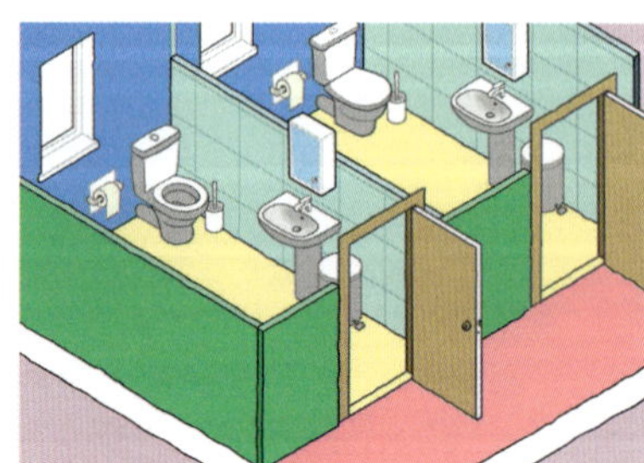

5 There are two toilets.

6 There's a balcony.

**I can describe my home or dream home.**

## 9 Things in a room

▶ SB, p. 56

a) Look at the pictures. Write the seven words in the puzzle.

1 
2 
3 
4 
5 
6 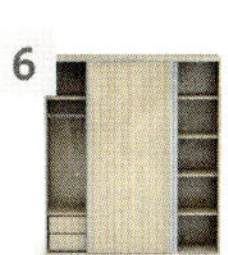
7 

8
1 CHAIR
2 COMPUTER
3 SOFA
4 SHELVES
5 MIRROR
6 WARDROBE
7 WINDOW

b) What is the word number 8 in your puzzle?

cushion

Draw a picture of it in the box.

## ☒ 10 Oscar's room

▶ SB, p. 56

Oscar writes about his room. Write words 1–10 correctly.

My room is (1) quite small.
It's on the first (2) floor of our house.
In my room I have my (3) bed and a big brown wardrobe. My (4) clothes and (5) shoes are in the (6) wardrobe.
And I have a (7) desk and a chair too.
I have a computer, some (8) books and three (9) posters of my favourite stars.
And I have a nice new (10) lamp.

1 ITEUQ
2 OROFL
3 EDB
4 THEOLCS
5 OSHES
6 BOERDRAW
7 KESD
8 OBOKS
9 ERSTOPS
10 PLAM

▶ Early finisher 1, p. 37

I can describe my room.

## 11 Olivia's room

▶ More help, p. 38 ▶ SB, p. 58

Olivia is Oscar's sister. Here's a picture of her room.

a) Read sentences 1–6 and look at the picture. Put a tick (✓) in the box for the correct sentence(s) or an ✗ in the box for the wrong sentence(s).

b) Now correct the wrong sentences. Use *is / isn't* and *are / aren't*.

1 Olivia's shoes are on the bed. ☒
No, they aren't ! They're under the bed.

2 The chair is behind the desk. ☒
No, it isn't! It's in front of it/the desk.

3 Her cushions are red. ☑
______

4 There's a picture in front of her bed. ☒
No, there isn't! It's behind the sofa.

5 Her shelves are next to the door. ☒
No, they aren't! They're next to the window.

6 Her lamp is under the table. ☒
No, it isn't! It's/Her lamp is on the desk.

## 12 Questions and answers

▶ More help, p. 39 ▶ SB, p. 58

**First look at the answers. Then write the missing words in the questions and answers.**

1 Who is Olivia? – Olivia is Oscar's sister.
2 Where 's Oscar and Olivia's flat? – It's in Brighton.
3 What 's behind the flat? – A garden with a lot of trees.
4 Where 's Olivia's bedroom? – Next to the bathroom.
5 What 's Olivia's favourite thing in her room? – Her phone. ▶ Early finisher 2, p. 37

## 13 Reading A special person

▸ Digital help ▸ SB, p. 59

At school, in English, Oscar writes about a special person. He chooses one of his grandmas.

Read Oscar's text and the questions. First highlight the places in the text where you find the information for your answers. Then write the answers to the questions.

*My mum's mum has a house in Watford, near London. I love my grandma's house. It isn't very big, but it's quite old and really nice. The hall is cool – it has six doors! On the ground floor my grandma has a living room with a big window and you can see three big trees in her garden. We often eat in the garden because my grandma loves barbecues. There isn't a dining room, but when we eat in the house we eat in the kitchen.*

*My grandma lives alone, but she has a dog, Monty.*

*Monty is a funny animal and I like to play with him. He's very fast! Monty loves the big old sofa in my grandma's living room and he always wants to play with my shoes!*

*There are really nice neighbours on one side, but horrible neighbours on the other side. I'm a bit scared of the horrible neighbours. They're mean to my grandma. I don't like that.*

*When I'm at my grandma's house I have a room on the first floor, next to the bathroom. The room is always very tidy because when I'm not there, it's my grandma's office. In the room there are shelves with a lot of interesting books. My grandma loves reading. Her favourite books are history books.*

*My grandma is always kind to me and always has some chocolate for me when I come. She is a very special person for me.*

1 Is grandma's house modern? *No, (it's) quite old.*

2 What's special in the hall? *(It has) six doors.*

3 What is there in grandma's garden? *Three big trees.*

4 Are all the neighbours friendly? *No, (they aren't).*

5 Where is Oscar's room in grandma's house? *On the first floor, (next to the bathroom).*

6 What are on the shelves in grandma's office? *Interesting books.*

7 What are grandma's favourite books? *History books.*

8 Grandma always has something special for Oscar. What is it? *Chocolate.*

▸ Challenge 1, p. 39

## 14 READING Sunita and Ben

▶ SB, pp. 60–62

**Look at the story on pages 60–62 in your book. Answer the questions about the four parts.**

*The start of the story ...*

1 Where's Sunita at the start of the story? At home.

2 Is Sunita a fan of Ben? Yes, because he's funny / he's a great cook.

No, because his music is horrible.

3 Who loves Ben's music? Sunita's mum.

*In the dining room...*

4 What's true? Tick (✓) A or B.

A Nish and Sunita have a lot of homework. ☐ B Nish and Sunita think Ben's music is really bad. ☑

*Later in the living room ...*

5 What are two problems with Ben's music? It's bad and it's loud.

6 What's the end of the problem? (*two answers*)

And Ben can play different music.

Ben can use headphones.

*The end of the story (in Sunita's texts to Lily) ...*

7 Where can Sunita use some of Ben's music? In her video game.

## 15 READING All about Ben

▶ SB, pp. 60–62

**Write the missing words.**

Ben has a nice little flat with Willow. Ben is part of Sunita's family. He has an electric guitar. He can help Sunita with music for her video game.

## 16 READING Language in the text

▶ SB, pp. 60–62

**Find the opposites in the text.**

1 with other people – alone
2 loud – quiet
3 there – here
4 really great – horrible
5 bad – good
6 old – new
7 big – little
8 rude – polite

I can understand a problem and talk about it. 

## 17 Find the partners

**Draw lines.**

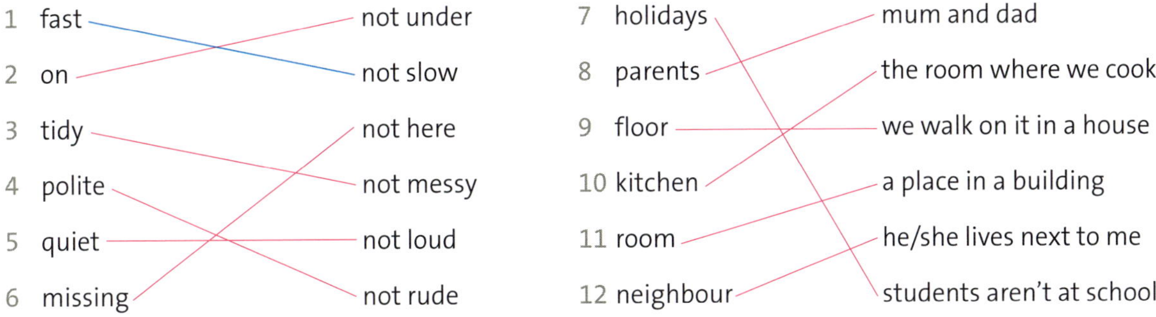

| | | | | |
|---|---|---|---|---|
| 1 fast | not under | | 7 holidays | mum and dad |
| 2 on | not slow | | 8 parents | the room where we cook |
| 3 tidy | not here | | 9 floor | we walk on it in a house |
| 4 polite | not messy | | 10 kitchen | a place in a building |
| 5 quiet | not loud | | 11 room | he/she lives next to me |
| 6 missing | not rude | | 12 neighbour | students aren't at school |

## 18 Words that are almost the same

**Write the right words in the sentences.**

1 quiet/quite — We live in a *quite* ______ small house in a *quiet* ______ part of Brighton.

2 four/for — I have *four* ______ chairs and some shelves *for* ______ my books.

3 two/too — And I have *two* ______ tables *too* ______.

4 red/read — I use my nice *red* ______ lamp when I *read* ______.

5 its/it's — My lamp is old, but *it's* ______ special. I like *its* ______ colour.

## 19 Listening and Speaking **Speak good English**

07 **a) Listen to these six words. What's special about the letters in blue?**

1 listen 2 answer 3 know
4 chocolate 5 interesting 6 two

**b) Look at the following sentences. Highlight the letters that you don't say.**

1 That's interesting, but it's also wrong.
2 What's the right answer?
3 My friends like walking and talking!
4 My grandma lives in a different building.
5 I know eight different people in this class.

08 **c) Listen to the sentences and repeat them.**

### I think English is:

not hard ☐ quite hard ☐
very hard ☐ fun ☐
interesting ☐ useful ☐

### My favourite page in Unit 2:

(page 53)

### Why:

(I like pets.)

### My favourite words:

dream
(cute)
(sweets)
(quite)

### Difficult words:

| to write: | to say: |
|---|---|
| neighbour | clothes |
| (daughter) | (mirror) |
| (quite) | (shelves) |
| (address) | (photographer) |
| (cushion) | (chocolate) |

### I remember:

Family: parents, (uncle, aunt, cousin, brother, sister, daughter, grandma, grandpa)

Rooms in the house: hall, (living room, kitchen, office, dining room, bathroom, bedroom)

Question words: who?, (where?, what?)

Where things are: under, (on, in front of, behind, next to)

Adjectives to describe people: rude, (polite, angry, messy, tidy, active, cute, funny)

### Learning English:

Complete the smileys: ☺ = I like it. 😐 = It's OK. ☹ = I don't like it.

Speaking ◯ Listening ◯ Viewing ◯
Writing ◯ Story ◯ Spelling ◯

## Early finisher 1 Word puzzles

Can you complete the puzzles? Write one letter in each box.

**a) Words to describe people and things**

| | | | | | | | | | |
|---|---|---|---|---|---|---|---|---|---|
| 1 | S | A | D | | | | | | |
| 2 | R | U | D | E | | | | | |
| 3 | A | L | O | N | E | | | | |
| 4 | H | U | N | G | R | Y | | | |
| 5 | P | A | S | S | I | V | E | | |
| 6 | F | R | I | E | N | D | L | Y | |
| 7 | D | I | F | F | I | C | U | L | T |

1 not happy
2 not polite
3 not with other people
4 when you want to eat
5 not active
6 not mean
7 hard

**b) Verbs**

| | | | | | | | | |
|---|---|---|---|---|---|---|---|---|
| 1 | E | A | T | | | | | |
| 2 | M | O | V | E | | | | |
| 3 | D | R | E | A | M | | | |
| 4 | A | N | S | W | E | R | | |
| 5 | B | E | R | I | G | H | T | |
| 6 | R | E | M | E | M | B | E | R |

1 have a sandwich or other food
2 go from here to there
3 see pictures when I'm asleep
4 after a question you ...
5 (*two words*) not be wrong
6 think of a thing again

**c) Family – you choose the words!**

| | | | | | | | | |
|---|---|---|---|---|---|---|---|---|
| 1 | A | U | N | T | | | | |
| 2 | U | N | C | L | E | | | |
| 3 | S | I | S | T | E | R | | |
| 4 | B | R | O | T | H | E | R | |
| 5 | D | A | U | G | H | T | E | R |

**d) Things in a bedroom – you choose!**

| | | | | | | | | |
|---|---|---|---|---|---|---|---|---|
| 1 | S | O | F | A | | | | |
| 2 | C | H | A | I | R | | | |
| 3 | M | I | R | R | O | R | | |
| 4 | S | H | E | L | V | E | S | |
| 5 | W | A | R | D | R | O | B | E |

## Early finisher 2 A message in code

Sunita is at school. Her phone buzzes. It's a message from Lily – a message in code! Can you write the message?

| |
|---|
| +^. ^ ∗{ ]∗¤↕ ⌂–/ ╕>+––]. ¤↕]] ¤+↕ ¤↕¤>+↕/ {ω |
| Hi. I AM LATE FOR SCHOOL. TELL THE TEACHER MY |
| /∗±±^¤ ^╕ ]–╕¤ ^ῴ ¤+↕ "∗/<↕ῴ. ¤+∗ῴ=╕. |
| RABBIT IS LOST IN THE GARDEN. THANKS. |

| ∗ | | | | ↕ | | | + | ^ | | | ] | | | – | | / | ╕ | ¤ | ω |
|---|---|---|---|---|---|---|---|---|---|---|---|---|---|---|---|---|---|---|---|
| A | B | C | D | E | F | G | H | I | J | K | L | M | N | O | P | R | S | T | Y |

▸ Check

## More help 11 Olivia's room

▶ WB, p. 32 ▶ SB, p. 58

Olivia is Oscar's sister. Here's a picture of her room.

a) Read sentences 1-6 and look at the picture. Put a tick (✓) in the box for the correct sentence(s) or an ✗ in the box for the wrong sentence(s).

b) Now correct the wrong sentences. The words in the boxes can help you.

| is • isn't • are • aren't |
|---|

| behind • in front of • next to • on • under |
|---|

1 Olivia's shoes are on the bed. ✗

No, they aren't! They're under the bed.

2 The chair is behind the desk. ✗

No, it isn't! It's in front of it/the desk.

3 Her cushions are red. ✓

4 There's a picture in front of her bed. ✗

No, there isn't! It's behind the sofa.

5 Her shelves are next to the door. ✗

No, they aren't! They're next to the window.

6 Her lamp is under the table. ✗

No, it isn't! It's/Her lamp is on the desk.

## More help 12 Questions and answers

► WB, p. 32 ► SB, p. 58

Look at the answers. Then write the missing question words.

1 Who is Olivia? – Olivia is Oscar's sister.
2 Where 's Oscar and Olivia's flat? – It's in Brighton.
3 What 's behind the flat? – A garden with a lot of trees.
4 Where 's Olivia's bedroom? – Next to the bathroom.
5 What 's Olivia's favourite thing in her room? – Her phone.

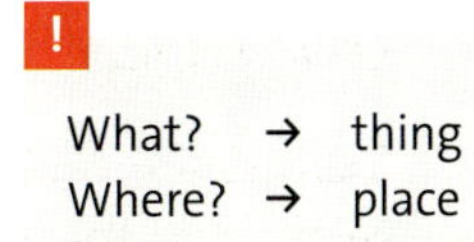
!
What? → thing
Where? → place
Who? → person

## Challenge 1 WRITING A special person

► Digital help ► WB, p. 33

Write about your grandma or grandpa or another special person.
Write about the person's house or flat, pets, hobbies, etc.

It's good to use and change sentences in Oscar's text.
Example:
We ~~often~~ eat in the ~~garden~~ because ~~my grandma loves barbecues.~~
We always eat in the living room because there isn't a dining room.

Start like this:

*My special person is ...*

*He/She has a house/flat in ...*

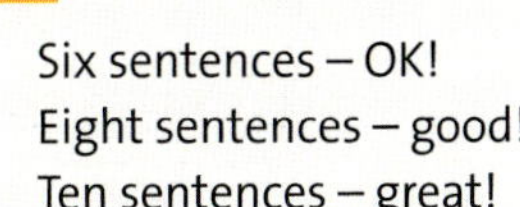
Six sentences – OK!
Eight sentences – good!
Ten sentences – great!

# Unit 3
# My day

## 1 Oscar

a) Write Oscar's sentences (1–5).

**!**

I go to ... by ...
I walk to ...

▸ SB, p. 81

I go to a lot of places ....

| | |
|---|---|
| | 3 Picture: D<br>beach • bike • by • go • I • the • to<br>I go to the beach by bike. |
| 1 Picture: C<br>by • go • grandma's • house • I • my • to • train<br>I go to my grandma's house by train. | 4 Picture: B<br>friend's • house • I • my • to • walk<br>I walk to my friend's house. |
| 2 Picture: E<br>by • car • dad's • flat • go • I • my • to<br>I go to my dad's flat by car. | 5 Picture: A<br>bus • by • go • I • school • to<br>I go to school by bus. |

b) Match the pictures (A–E) to the sentences (1–5). Write the letters in the boxes.

A 

B 

C 

D 

E 

I can talk about my school journey.

## 2 Listening Numbers

▶ Digital help ▶ SB, p. 82

09–12

a) • Choose five numbers: 10 15 20 25 30 35 40 45 50 55 60. Write them in the boxes.
• Play the game in groups. Listen. When you hear your numbers, cross them out (~~15~~).
• When you have all five numbers, shout "Here!". The game ends – you win!

Game 1

| | | | | |
|---|---|---|---|---|
| | | | | |

Game 3

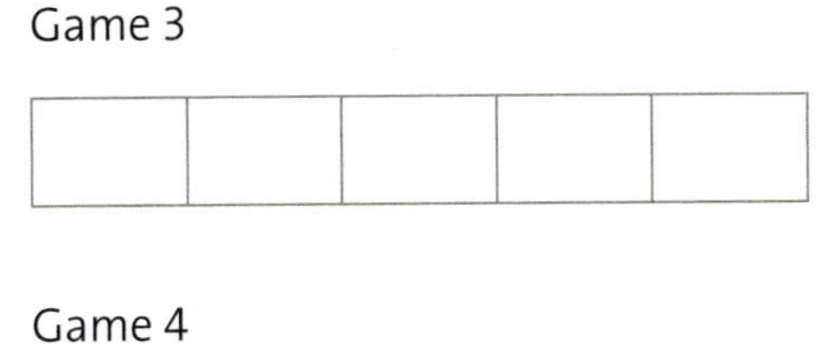

| | | | | |
|---|---|---|---|---|
| | | | | |

Game 2

| | | | | |
|---|---|---|---|---|
| | | | | |

Game 4

| | | | | |
|---|---|---|---|---|
| | | | | |

13

b) Listen. (Circle) the right number.

1 34/(43) 2 (25)/52 3 (64)/46 4 54/(45)
5 42/(24) 6 36/(63) 7 (26)/62 8 53/(35)

## 3 Language Simple present Oscar's Saturday

▶ SB, p. 84

Erklär-film

Write a sentence for each picture.

| | | |
|---|---|---|
| He | does | a shower. |
| | gets | TV. |
| | gets | up. |
| | goes | dressed. |
| | has | his sister to the park. |
| | makes | his homework. |
| | takes | to football training. |
| | watches | a snack. |

1  He gets up.

2  He has a shower.

3  He gets dressed.

4  He goes to football training.

5  He makes a snack.

6  He takes his sister to the park.

7  He watches TV.

8 

He does his homework.

## 4 LANGUAGE Simple present Oscar's mum and stepdad

▶ SB, p. 84

a) Find the times. Write sentences about Saturday. Write the verbs in the simple present.

*Be careful!*
*does / goes / has / tidies*

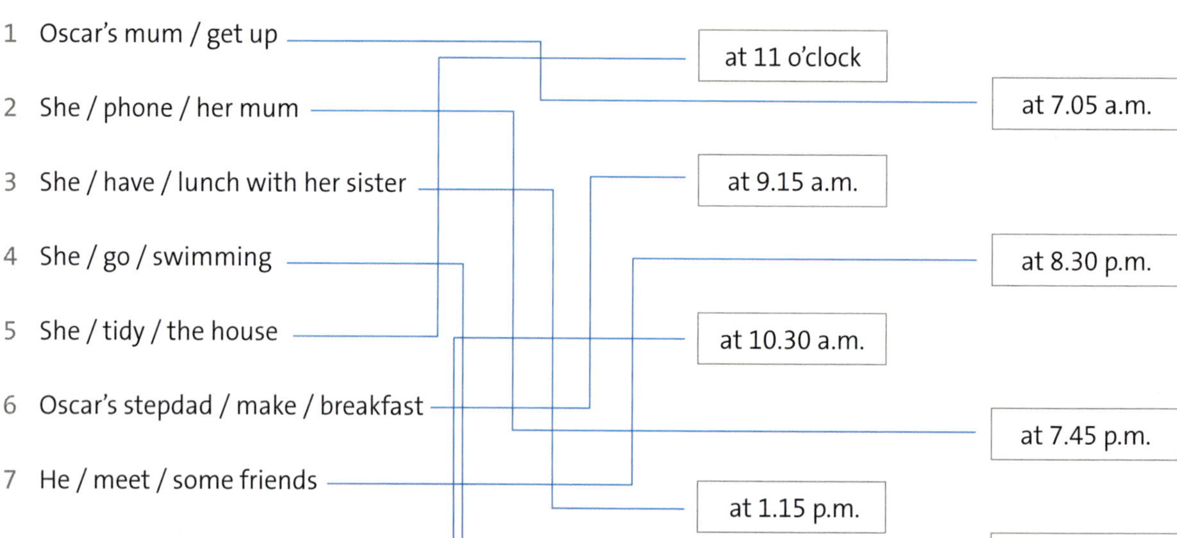


1 Oscar's mum gets up at 7.05 a.m.
2 She phones her mum at 7.45 p.m.
3 She has lunch with her sister at 1.15 p.m.
4 She goes swimming at 7.25 a.m.
5 She tidies the house at 11 o'clock.
6 Oscar's stepdad makes breakfast at 9.15 a.m.
7 He meets some friends at 8.30 p.m.
8 He does the shopping at 10.30 a.m.

b) Check with your partner.

## 5 LANGUAGE Simple present Oscar's friend Ling

▸ More help, p. 52 ▸ SB, p. 84

**a) Ling tells Oscar about her week. Circle the correct verb.**

| | | Time |
|---|---|---|
| 1 | On weekdays I **get / gets** up at 7 a.m. and I **have / has** a shower. | 7.05 a.m. |
| 2 | My mum **make / makes** breakfast for me and my brothers. | 7.25 a.m. |
| 3 | I **walk / walks** to school and my parents **goes / go** to work by car. | 8.10 a.m. |
| 4 | But on Sunday we **make / makes** breakfast for Mum and Dad. | 9.45 a.m. |
| 5 | My grandma **come / comes** to our house. | 11.30 a.m. |
| 6 | She **make / makes** my favourite lunch! | 1 o'clock |
| 7 | Then we all **play / plays** games. It's nice! | |
| 8 | I **love / loves** Sundays! | |

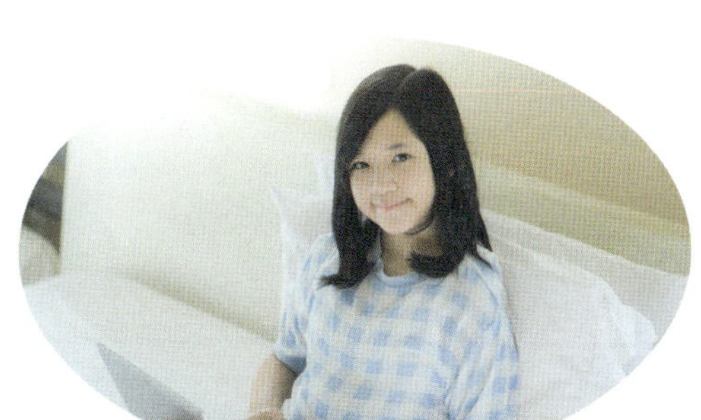

14 **b) Listen and check your answers.**

14 **c) Listen again and write the times.**

## 6 LANGUAGE Simple present Kitty, the cat

▸ More help, p. 52 ▸ SB, p. 85

**Ling's cat Kitty talks about her day!**
**Choose the right verbs. Write the verbs in the simple present.**

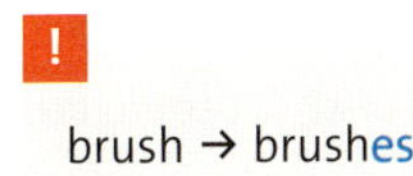
! brush → brushes

| brush • eat • get • go • have • make • play • watch |
|---|

I (1) get ______ up at 6 o'clock, but the people are all asleep.
The mum (2) makes ______ my breakfast at 7 o'clock,
and Ling (3) plays ______ a game with me before school.

In the afternoon, I often (4) watch ______ seagulls in the garden.
The big seagull (5) has ______ a lot of friends.
Then I (6) go ______ back to bed.

In the evening, I (7) eat ______ my dinner.
Then Ling (8) brushes ______ me – prrrr!

I can describe my daily routine. ✓

## 7 Sports and hobbies

▸ More help, p. 53 ▸ SB, p. 86

a) Look at the pictures. Write the words.

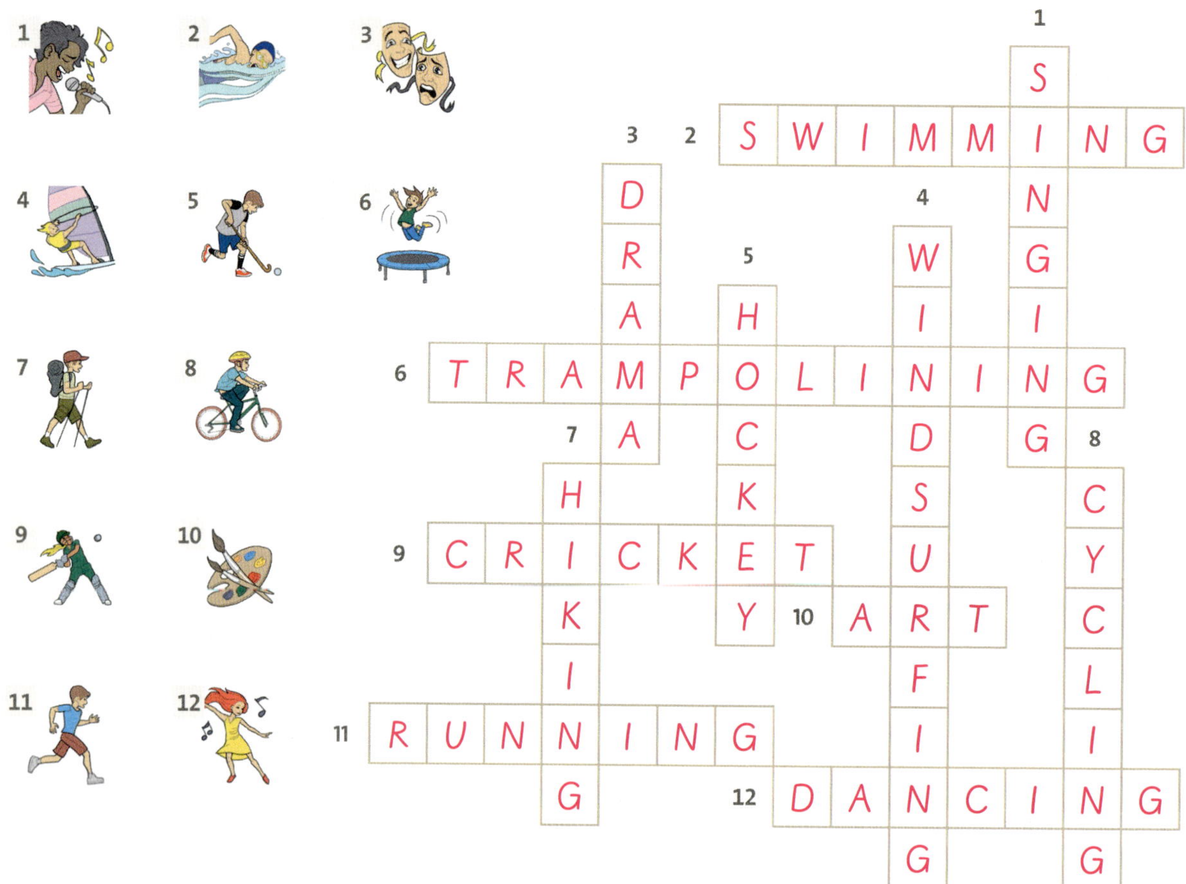

b) Write about six sports / hobbies: ***I like … / I love … / I don't like …***

*I love tennis* ***and*** *I like football,* ***but*** *I don't like …*

## 8 Alphabet sports and hobbies

▸ Digital help

Write the alphabet A–Z in your exercise book.
How many[1] letters can you write a sport or hobby for?

A – art
B – …
C – …

You can work with a partner. Look at the dictionary in your book for help.

[1] **how many?** *wie viele?*

## 9 Do you go running?

▸ SB, p. 87

Read the sentences. Write the names in the right order.

Ben | Reeta | Jack | Holly | Mo

## 10 READING Online chat room

▸ SB, p. 89

Read the messages. Tick (✓) the hobbies.

Words in the messages are different!
music – *singing*

*Hi. I'm Lexi and I'm 11 years old. I'm from Liverpool, but I live in Hove now. I love singing. At the weekend I always play football with my friends. What about you? Tell me about your hobbies!*

*Hello. My name is Jaden and I'm 12. I live next to the sea. I have lots of hobbies. When the wind is good, my mum and I sometimes go windsurfing. It's great! I like reading, too – I love science-fiction.*

*My name is Rose. I have a big sister, a little brother and two cats. I go to a hockey club after school with my friend. I like it – the other kids are nice. My dad and I often go cycling at the weekend.*

*Hey! I'm Billy. I'm 12 years old and I live in Brighton. I really like drawing and I go to a club after school. I often go swimming in the sea too – and my dog always goes swimming with me!*

*Hi. I'm Becky and I'm 10. After school, I always play my guitar in my bedroom. I sometimes play table tennis with my friends. My friend Joel has a table in his garage.*

| | art | books | sport with a ball | water sports | music | bike |
|---|---|---|---|---|---|---|
| Lexi | | | ✓ | | ✓ | |
| Jaden | | ✓ | | ✓ | | |
| Rose | | | ✓ | | | ✓ |
| Billy | ✓ | | | ✓ | | |
| Becky | | | ✓ | | ✓ | |

## 11 LISTENING Radio interviews on the beach

15

► SB, p. 89

Listen to the people. Find the right picture.
Write the letter (A–H) and *sometimes* / *often* / *always*.

Listen again if you need to.

1 Picture: D always
2 Picture: B often
3 Picture: F sometimes
4 Picture: H always
5 Picture: A sometimes
6 Picture: E often
7 Picture: C always
8 Picture: G often

A 
B 
C 
D 
E 
F
G
H

## 12 Free time

► SB, p. 89

a) Write five sentences about your activities – four are right, one is wrong.

| | | | |
|---|---|---|---|
| I | like<br>don't like | drama reading singing windsurfing trampolining art music ... | |
| | always<br>sometimes<br>often<br>rarely<br>never | play | basketball the guitar computer games table tennis ... |
| | | go | cycling hiking running swimming dancing to film club ... |
| | | watch TV | |
| | | listen to music | |

b) Your partner guesses which sentence is wrong.

c) WALK AROUND Say sentences to other students. How many are right?

*You sometimes play football.*

*Wrong! I never play football.*

► Challenge 1, p. 53 ► Early finisher 1, p. 51

I can talk about my free time.

## 13 LISTENING Friends want to meet

16 ▸ SB, p. 90

a) Listen to these friends. Right (✓) or wrong (✗)?

b) Listen again and correct the sentences.

| | | | ✓ / ✗ | |
|---|---|---|---|---|
| A | 1 | Max is free on ~~Sunday~~. | ✗ | Saturday |
| | 2 | Anna wants to go to the beach. | ✓ | |
| | 3 | Their meeting is at ~~11.30~~. | ✗ | 10.30 |
| B | 1 | Lucy has drama club on Saturday. | ✓ | |
| | 2 | Dev wants to go to ~~hiking~~. | ✗ | cycling |
| | 3 | Their meeting is at ~~Lucy's house~~. | ✗ | the park |

## 14 SPEAKING Are you free?

▸ Digital help ▸ SB, p. 91

**Look at the diagram. Act four conversations with a partner. Use words from boxes 1–4. You can use your own ideas too! Swap roles.**

A Are you free on (1)? Let's (2).

B Good idea! I'd love to. → A Great!

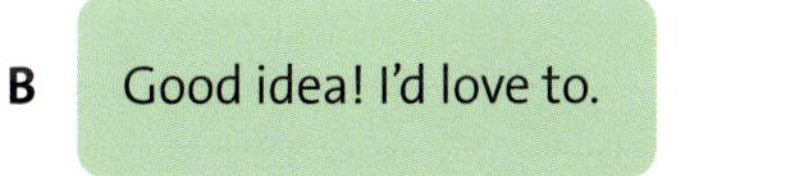

B Sorry, I can't. I'm busy. → A What about (1)?

B OK. Let's meet at (3) on (1).

A Where? At (4)?

B OK. See you then.

(1) Friday / Saturday / Sunday / Monday / ...

(2) go hiking / go swimming / go to the cafe / play table tennis / watch a film / ...

(3) 2 o'clock / 2.30 / 3 o'clock / 3.30 / ...

(4) my house / flat / your house / flat / ...

I can make plans to meet friends. ✓

## 15 VIEWING What do they say?

► SB, p. 95

**Watch the film. What do these people say? Tick (✓) the right sentence.**

| | | | | | |
|---|---|---|---|---|---|
| Part 1 | Daisy: | ☑ | How can I do street music? | ☐ | Where can I do street music? |
| Part 2 | Gloria: | ☐ | You're so sad! | ☑ | You're so quiet! |
| Part 3 | Amal: | ☑ | I can't play for six weeks! | ☐ | I can't play for six days! |
| Part 4 | Emir: | ☑ | Well, I can try. | ☐ | Well, I can't try. |
| Part 5 | Gloria: | ☐ | I sing with my friends at school. | ☑ | I sing in a group at school. |
| Part 6 | Jenny: | ☐ | Street music? On a Sunday morning? | ☑ | Street music? On a Saturday morning? |

## 16 VIEWING You can act

► SB, p. 95

a) **Watch Part 1 (00:39 to 01:15) again and read the text. Listen to *how* they say the sentences.**

**Emir** You want me to play my next football match with a pair of underpants on my head?!? Like this? Are you crazy[1]?!?

**Daisy** And you want me to play street music? Street music?!? In front of people? I can't sing. I can't play a musical instrument! How can I do street music?

**Emir** Dare or no dare?

**Daisy** Dare!

b) SPEAKING **Now act the part with a partner. Act it lots of times so you're really good!**

You can watch again and say the sentences after Emir and Daisy.

## 17 What do you think?

► SB, p. 95

**Write what you think about the dares. You can use words from the box.**

a good idea • great • mean • really funny • stupid • too hard • weird • ...

1 I think Emir's dare for Daisy is ______________________

2 I think Daisy's ______________________

[1] **crazy** *verrückt*

## 18 Word groups

a) Write the words in the right groups.

b) Write one more word in each list.

| afternoon | aunt | bike | car |
|---|---|---|---|
| evening | husband | letter | lunchtime |
| newspaper | son | story | train |

| Things you read | People in the family | Transport | Times in the day |
|---|---|---|---|
| letter | aunt | bike | afternoon |
| newspaper | husband | car | evening |
| story | son | train | lunchtime |
| (book) | (sister) | (bus) | (morning) |

## 19 Useful phrases

Oscar asks Ling to go to the beach. Complete the useful phrases with words from the box.

about • done • let's • much • of • shame • sorry

**Oscar** Are you free on Sunday? Let's go to the beach.

**Ling** Sorry, I'm busy. I have a lot of homework.

**Oscar** That's a shame. What about Saturday?

**Ling** Sorry, I can't. But don't be sorry for me – I'm in a singing competition. It's the final!

**Oscar** That's great! Well done!

**Ling** Thank you so much!

## 20 SPEAKING Speak English well

a) Look at the words.
Find the 'Zane' words [eɪ]. Circle them.
Find the 'Dad' words [æ]. Underline them.

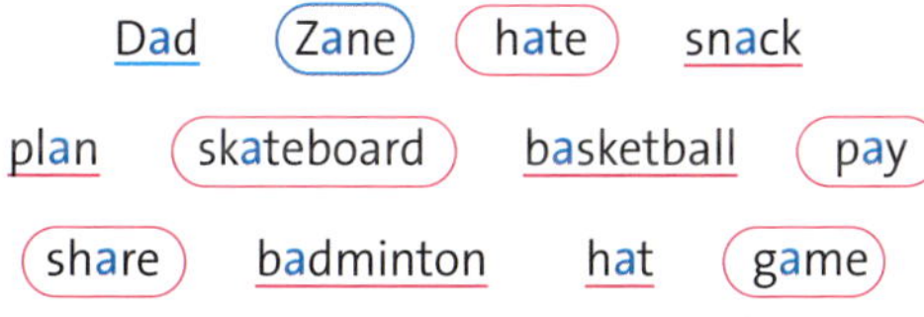

Dad (Zane) (hate) snack
plan (skateboard) basketball (pay)
(share) badminton hat (game)

Zane
[eɪ] in your dictionary

Dad
[æ] in your dictionary

17 b) Listen and check. Repeat the words.

**My favourite words:**

o'clock
(lunchtime)
(singing)
(secret)

| Difficult words: | to write | to say |
|---|---|---|
| teeth | ☐ | ☑ |
| (competition) | ☐ | ☐ |
| (journey) | ☐ | ☐ |
| (sometimes) | ☐ | ☐ |

**Useful phrases:**

Thank you so much. (Well done!)
(That's a shame!) (I'd love to.)

**I remember:**

How people go to school: by car, (by bus, by train, by bike, walk)

In the morning: I get up, (I have a shower, I brush my teeth, I get dressed, I eat breakfast, I go to school)

Some hobbies and activities: trampolining, (drama, cycling, singing, hiking, reading, art)

Some things I do: I watch ... / I go ... / I like ... / ... (I watch TV, I go swimming, I play computer games, I like music)

How often: always, (sometimes, often, rarely, never)

**My favourite exercises in Unit 3 in the workbook:**

Write the exercise numbers: __________

**My progress[1] in English:**

- ☐ great!
- ☐ OK
- ☐ some things are quite difficult

*Some things are difficult? You can ask your teacher or a friend for help!*

[1] **progress** *Fortschritt*

Early finisher 1 **Twelve different girls** ▸ Check

a) WRITING Choose two girls. Look at the pictures for 30 seconds, then close the workbook. What can you remember about each girl? Write sentences in your exercise book. Use the verbs from the box.

*She plays cricket. She ...*

go • have • like ♥ • live in a • play • watch • ...

b) Partner game: Partner A says four sentences about one girl.
Then partner B looks at the pictures. How fast can partner B find the right girl?
Then swap.

Eva

Orla

Pari

Pippa

Rosa

Hannah

Penny

Aarna

Carmen

Tamara

Tess

Noor

## More help 5 LANGUAGE Simple present Oscar's friend Ling

▶WB, p. 43 ▶SB, p. 84

a) Ling tells Oscar about her week. (Circle) the correct verb.

| | | Time |
|---|---|---|
| 1 | On weekdays I (get) / gets up at 7 a.m. and I (have) / has a shower. | (7.05) / 7.10 a.m. |
| 2 | My mum make / (makes) breakfast for me and my brothers. | 7.20 / (7.25) a.m. |
| 3 | I (walk) / walks to school and my parents goes / (go) to work by car. | (8.10) / 8.20 a.m. |
| 4 | But on Sunday we (make) / makes breakfast for Mum and Dad. | 9.30 / (9.45) a.m. |
| 5 | My grandma come / (comes) to our house. | 11.15 / (11.30) a.m. |
| 6 | She make / (makes) my favourite lunch! | 12 / (1) o'clock |
| 7 | Then we all (play) / plays games. It's nice! | |
| 8 | I (love) / loves Sundays! | |

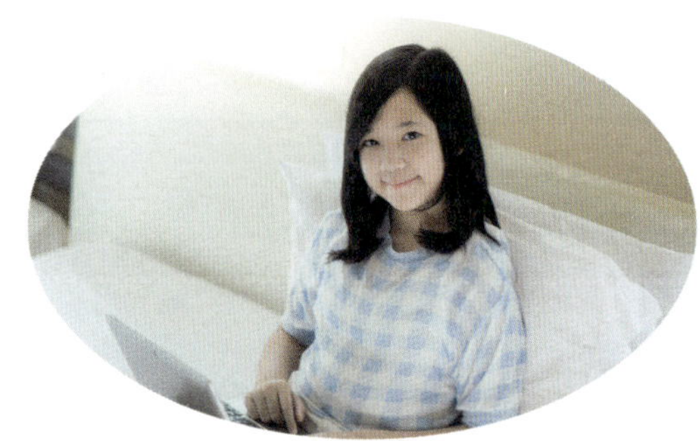

14 b) Listen and check your answers.

14 c) Listen again and (circle) the correct times.

## More help 6 LANGUAGE Simple present Kitty, the cat

▶WB, p. 43 ▶SB, p. 85

Ling's cat Kitty talks about her day!
Write the verbs in the simple present.

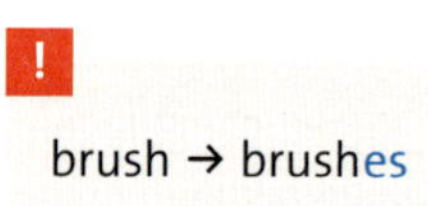


I (1 get) *get* up at 6 o'clock, but the people are all asleep. The mum (2 make) *makes* my breakfast at 7 o'clock, and Ling (3 play) *plays* a game with me before school.

In the afternoon, I often (4 watch) *watch* seagulls in the garden. The big seagull (5 have) *has* a lot of friends. Then I (6 go) *go* back to bed.

In the evening, I (7 eat) *eat* my dinner. Then Ling (8 brush) *brushes* me – prrrr!

## More help 7 Sports and hobbies

▸ WB, p. 44 ▸ SB, p. 86

a) Look at the pictures. Write the words.

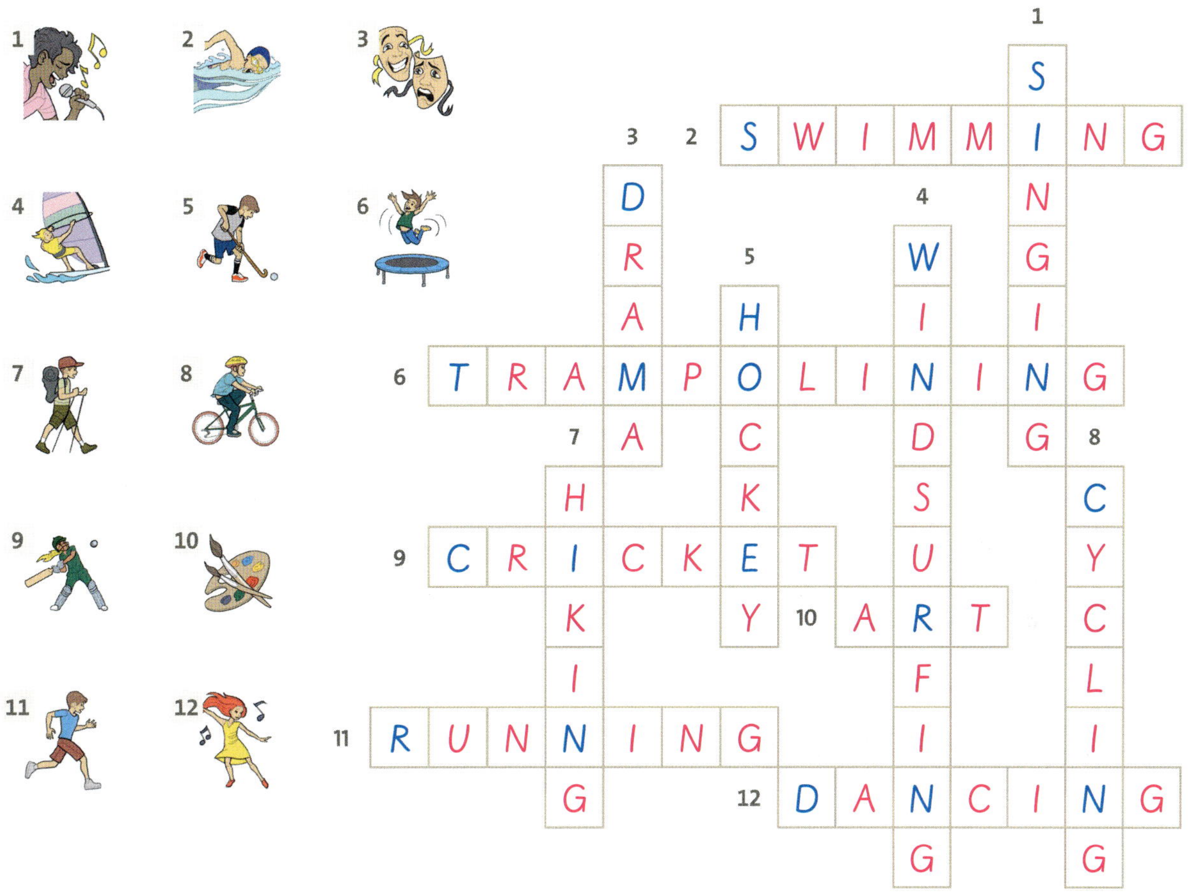


## Challenge 1 A person you know

▸ WB, p. 46

a) WRITING Choose a person you know (friend/family). How many things can you write about him/her? Use the ideas below.

name | how old | town | character | favourite things | family | animals | house | bedroom | hobbies | ...

Write on paper and put it on the classroom wall.

*I want to tell you about my cousin. Her name is Johanna and she's 9 years old. She lives in Berlin ...*

b) MEDIATION Your friend wants to write about her brother. Write her sentences in English.

1 Er gewinnt viele Wettbewerbe. *He wins lots of competitions.*

2 Sein Schlafzimmer ist immer unordentlich. *His bedroom is always messy.*

3 Er ist nett und hilft Menschen. *He is nice and (he) helps people.*

▸ Check 

## 1 Adjectives[1]

a) Match the opposites[2]. Draw lines. Use different colours. ▸ Digital help

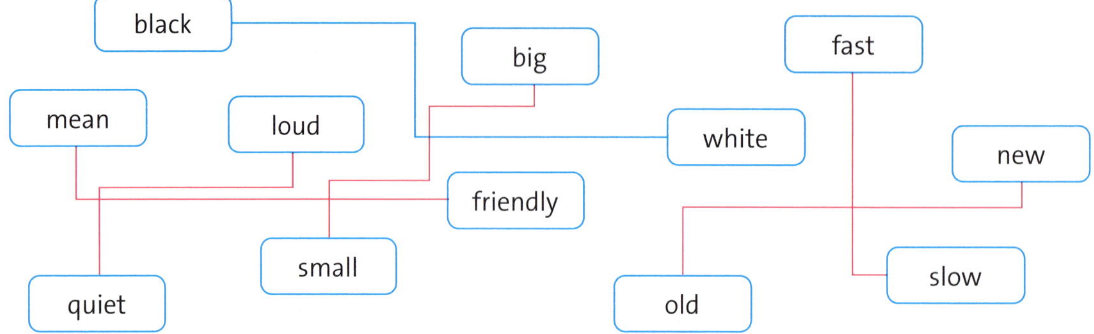


b) Write four more words to talk about people / animals / things.

*(active, busy, cute, messy, polite, special, ...)*

## 2 Colour maths

Write the correct colours.

1 red + white = *pink*

2 blue + yellow = *green*

3 black + white = *grey*

4 red + blue = *purple*

5 red + yellow = *orange*

6 red + yellow + blue = *brown*

## 3 Tia's hamsters

Read sentences 1–8. Look at the picture of Tia's bedroom on page 55. Find Tia's hamsters. Write the correct letters.

1 Pip is a small, black hamster. It's on Tia's bed. *B*

2 Pop is a white hamster. It's on the floor, next to the wardrobe. *E*

3 Hammy is under the bed. It's scared! *F*

4 Speedy is a big, brown hamster. It's on a cushion on the floor. *A*

5 Rambo is on the floor, next to the mirror. *G*

6 Cookie is a brown hamster. It's on the shelf next to the window. *H*

7 Blackie is a black hamster. It's on the wardrobe! *C*

8 Muffin is on the chair, next to the desk. *D*

[1] **adjective** *Adjektiv* [2] **opposite** *Gegenteil*

▸ Check

Erklär-
film

## 4 Tia's hobbies

Look at Tia's room again. Can you find: ☐ 4 + hobbies / ☒ 8 hobbies? Write sentences.

*She plays table tennis. / She likes table tennis.*

*She likes reading. / She likes books.*

*She goes swimming. / She likes swimming.*

*She likes drawing. / She likes art.*

*She plays the guitar. / She likes music.*

*She plays computer games. / She likes computer games.*

*She does trampolining. / She likes trampolining.*

*She goes cycling. / She likes cycling.*

**!** Remember: *she*... +*s*
*like* → *she likes*

▸ Check

Unit4

# Where I live

## 1 Places in a city

► SB, p. 111

a) Write the eight places.

A

This is a
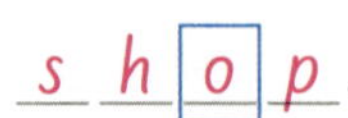
s h o p.

B

This is a
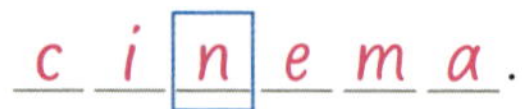
c i n e m a.

C

Here is a

s t r e e t.

D

This is a
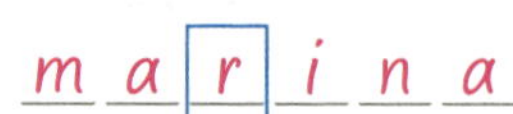
m a r i n a.

E

This is a
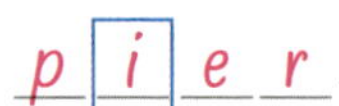
p i e r.

F

Here are nice

g a r d e n s.

G

This is a

s c h o o l.

H

And here is the

b e a c h.

b) Answer the question.

*The letters in the boxes in a) spell the name of a city in England. What's the name of the city?*

Brighton

## 2 Activities in Brighton

► SB, p. 111

Write the verbs. Use the verbs in the box.

eat • go • hear • play • practise • understand • watch

You ...

| | |
|---|---|
| watch | films. |
| eat | fish and chips. |
| play | games. |
| go | bowling. |
| practise | new skills. |
| hear | street music. |
| understand | information. |

*Mmmm! Nice!*

I can understand information about Brighton.

## 3 Reading Lily and the Whitehawk Estate

▸ Digital help ▸ SB, p. 112

**Read the text on page 112 in your student's book. Then read sentences 1–8. Are the sentences true (T) or false (F)?**

1 There's a place where you can buy things on the estate. 

2 Lily sometimes cycles to the town centre. 

3 The activities at the youth centre on the Whitehawk Estate are boring. 

4 Lily's sister lives in a different place with her husband. 

5 The sports centre is great because it has parkour. 

6 Lily often goes to the fields with her dad. 

7 Not everybody on the Whitehawk Estate puts rubbish in the bins. 

8 Lily thinks noise is sometimes a problem on the estate. 

## 4 Listening Our neighbourhoods

18

▸ More help, p. 68 ▸ SB, p. 113

a) **Five students in class 7C talk about their neighbourhoods. Listen. What do they talk about? Put a tick (✓) in the right boxes.**

| | estate | shops | youth centre | fields | noise | rubbish |
|---|---|---|---|---|---|---|
| Fatima | | ✓ | | ✓ | | |
| Finley | ✓ | | ✓ | | ✓ | |
| Hannah | | ✓ | | | | ✓ |
| Ivy | ✓ | ✓ | | ✓ | | |
| Syed | ✓ | | | ✓ | | |

b) **Listen again and circle the right words.**

1 Fatima says the people in her neighbourhood are **friendly / unfriendly**.

2 Finley says there is a lot of **noise / rubbish** in his neighbourhood.

3 Hannah says the streets in her neighbourhood are **clean / dirty**.

4 Ivy says her neighbourhood is **interesting / boring**.

5 Syed says there are some **big / small** sports fields on his estate.

## 5 LANGUAGE Simple present: negative sentences School

▸ SB, p. 114

a) **Read about school in Britain. Then write about school in Germany. Put the words in blue in the right order.**

| | |
|---|---|
| | |
| 1 School often starts at 8.50 am. | School doesn't start at 8.50 am.<br>**start / at 8.50 am / doesn't / school** |
| 2 Most students have a uniform. | Students don't have a uniform.<br>**have / a uniform / students / don't** |
| 3 The school day often starts with assembly. | The school day doesn't start with assembly.<br>**the school day / start with / doesn't / assembly** |
| 4 All students have lunch at school. | Some students don't have lunch at school.<br>**some students / at school / have lunch / don't** |
| 5 All students have lessons after lunch. | Some students don't have lessons after lunch.<br>**some students / have lessons / don't / after lunch** |
| 6 Students often play cricket. | Students don't play cricket.<br>**play / cricket / students / don't** |

b) **Now write about the students at Varndean School. Write *doesn't* or *don't*.**

Lily and Noah (1) don't walk to school because they (2) don't live near Varndean. Lily and her family (3) don't have a car. So Lily (4) doesn't go to school by car like Noah. She goes by bike. Zane (5) doesn't go to school by bike like Lily. He walks. School ends at 3.05, but a lot of students (6) don't go home then. Lily sometimes goes to Homework Club, but Zane (7) doesn't like Homework Club.

## 6 LANGUAGE Simple present: negative sentences Lily's neighbourhood

▶ SB, p. 114

**Now read about Lily's neighbourhood.**
**Circle the right form of the verb.**

1 Lily Hall **live / lives** on the Whitehawk Estate.
She doesn't **live / lives** near the beach.
2 She **go / goes** to Homework Club when her dad doesn't **come / comes** home before 5 o'clock.
3 Lily's neighbour **walk / walks** with his dog, but Lily doesn't **have / has** a dog.
4 Lily sometimes **walk / walks** in the fields with her dad, but he doesn't **walk / walks** very often.
5 Lily **like / likes** her estate because it doesn't **have / has** a lot of problems.
6 But she doesn't **like / likes** all the rubbish and all the cars in her estate.

*Remember!*
*My friend George **lives** in Sunita's house.*
*He doesn't **live** in Zane's house.*

## 7 LANGUAGE Simple present: negative sentences Alina

▶ SB, p. 114

**Read about Alina, a student at Varndean School. Then complete the sentences.**
**Use the verbs in blue in the negative.**

We live in a flat.
We don't live ________ in a house.

I have a cat.
I don't have ________ a dog.

My mum works in a school.
She doesn't work ________ in a shop.

I feel happy.
I don't feel ________ sad.

My sister lives in London.
She doesn't live ________ with us.

My dad plays football, but
he doesn't play ________ cricket.

I can describe my neighbourhood.

## 8 Places in town

▸ SB, p. 116

Highlight the eight places in town. Then write the eight places below.

▸ Early finisher 1, p. 67

| | | | |
|---|---|---|---|
| 1 *hospital* | 2 *library* | 3 *train station* | 4 *supermarket* |
| 5 *ice rink* | 6 *shopping centre* | 7 *museum* | 8 *stadium* |

Erklär-film

## 9 LANGUAGE Simple present: questions — Oscar and Chandra

▸ SB, p. 117

Chandra asks Oscar some questions and he answers. (Circle) the right word in the questions.

1. **Does / (Do)** you all live in a house? – No, we don't. We live in a flat.
2. **(Does) / Do** your stepdad live with you? – Yes, he does.
3. **(Does) / Do** your sister Olivia share a room? – No, she doesn't.
4. **Does / (Do)** you have posters in your room? – Yes, I do.
5. **(Does) / Do** your flat have a balcony? – Yes, it does.
6. **Does / (Do)** you like school? – No, I don't.

## 10 LANGUAGE Simple present: short answers — Now you

▸ SB, p. 117

**a)** Chandra asks you some questions. Write your answers. Use short answers.

1. Do you and your family live in a village? – *Yes, we do. / No, we don't.*
2. Do you like your neighbourhood? – *Yes, I do. / No, I don't.*
3. Does your school have a lot of students? – *Yes, it does. / No, it doesn't.*
4. Do you go to school by bike? – *Yes, I do. / No, I don't.*
5. Does your house or flat have a garden? – *Yes, it does. / No, it doesn't.*
6. Do you sometimes go bowling? – *Yes, I do. / No, I don't.*

**b)** SPEAKING Your partner asks you questions 1–6 and you answer. Then swap roles.

## 11 LANGUAGE Simple present: questions and short answers Devon and York

▸ SB, p. 117

**Partner B: Look at page 86.**
**Partner A: You want to know:**
**Is Devon a good place for a holiday in England?**

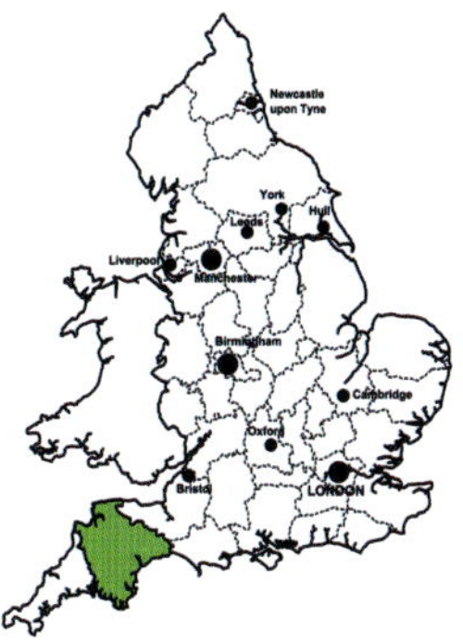


**a) Write the questions about Devon. Put the words in the right order.**

1 have / does / Devon / good windsurfing / ?
*Does Devon have good windsurfing?* ✓

2 many big cities / Devon / does / have / ?
*Does Devon have many big cities?* 

3 Devon / does / good beaches / have / ?
*Does Devon have good beaches?* 

4 for hiking / does / good places / have / Devon / ?
*Does Devon have good places for hiking?* 

5 good / does / Devon / have / football clubs / ?
*Does Devon have good football clubs?* 

**b) Now ask your partner about Devon. Put a tick (✓) in the box for yes, an ✗ for no.**

**c) Now look at the information about York.**

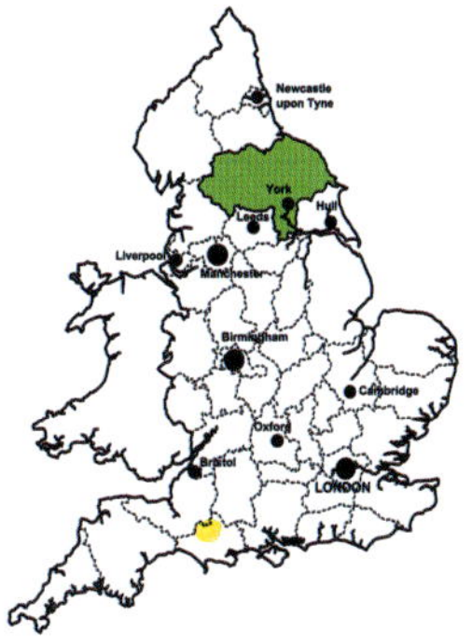


York has many old streets and buildings, interesting shops and a great train museum. But York doesn't have a marina, a beach or a big football stadium.

**d) Your partner asks you about York.**
**Answer your partner's questions. Use short answers:** ***Yes, it does. / No, it doesn't.***

**e) Now check your answers with your partner.**

## 12 LISTENING A weather map

19 ▶ SB, p. 120

a) Listen and look at the map. Cross out (~~cross out~~) the wrong weather symbol in each town.

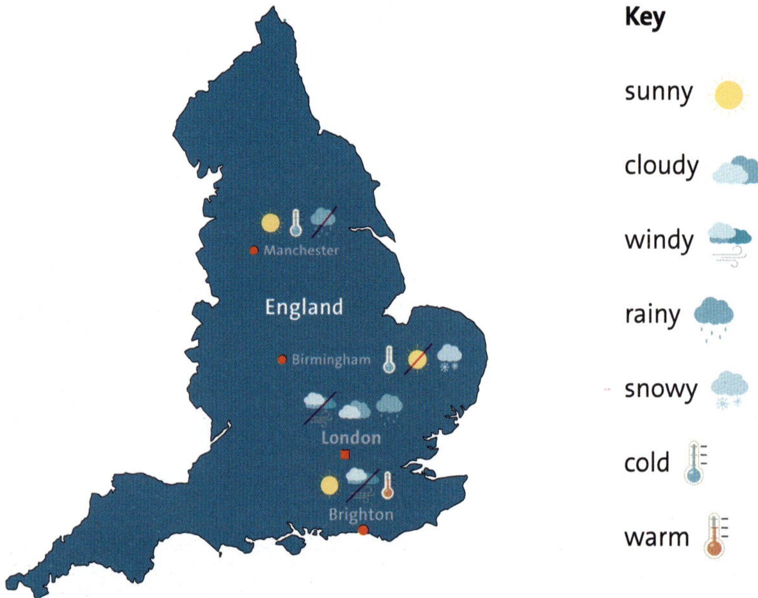


b) Listen again. Write the last word in each sentence.

1 In London it is rainy in the afternoon and evening.
2 In Brighton it's a great day for the beach.
3 In Manchester it's a different story.
4 In Birmingham it's a good day to be inside with a nice hot chocolate.

## 13 A funny old train

▶ SB, p. 121

**Brighton has the oldest electric train in the world. Match questions 1–7 with answers A–G.**

1 Where does the train travel? D
2 When does it open? G
3 How long is the journey? A
4 Where does the journey start? E
5 What does the journey cost? B
6 How often do the trains go? F
7 Does the train take dogs? C

A *It's very short! There are only three stops.*
B *£3.95 or £2.45 for girls and boys up to 15.*
C *Yes, it does, and the dogs travel free.*
D *Next to the sea.*
E *At Aquarium Station.*
F *Every 15 minutes.*
G *At 11.30 on Monday and Wednesday, and at 10.30 on other days.*

## 14 A great place to work

▸ SB, p. 121

a) Oscar writes about his stepdad's work for school. Read his text and the brochure.

My stepdad Kevin has a great job. He helps visitors in Thorpe Park, a fantastic fun park near London with great rollercoasters. Visitors can travel at 80 miles per hour (128 kilometres per hour) on Stealth. Or they can travel upside down on Vortex. My stepdad goes to work at 6.45 am, but he likes his work because he can sometimes ride on Stealth and Vortex when the visitors go home.

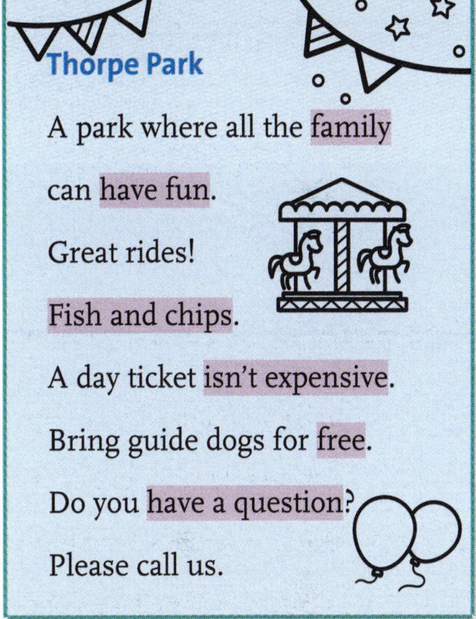


b) Highlight the words in the text and brochure that mean:

1 people who come to the park
2 go fast
3 head down
4 parents with sons and daughters
5 have a great time
6 hot food
7 doesn't cost a lot
8 don't pay
9 want to ask something

Erklär-film

c) LANGUAGE **Simple present: *wh*-questions**
Write the questions.

▸ More help, p. 69

1 Where does Kevin work? – He works at Thorpe Park.
2 What does Kevin do? – He helps the visitors.
3 How fast do visitors travel on *Stealth*? – They travel at 80 miles per hour.
4 How do visitors travel on *Vortex*? – They travel upside down.
5 When does Kevin go to work? – He goes to work at 6.45.
6 Why does Kevin like his job? – Because he can sometimes go on *Stealth* and *Vortex*.

▸ Challenge 1, p. 69

## 15 READING Tell the story

▸ SB, pp. 122–124

**Look at the story on pages 122–124 in your book. Then match the questions 1–6 with the answers A–F.**

| | | |
|---|---|---|
| 1 What does Lily do? | C | A He phones Lily's mum. |
| 2 What does Noah do? | E | B He finds a ring. |
| 3 What do the people on the estate do? | F | C She makes a poster. |
| 4 What does Buddy do? | B | D They give the youth centre some money. |
| 5 What does Davy do? | A | E He brings his dog. |
| 6 What do Davy's grandparents do? | D | F They clean up the estate. |

## ☒ 16 READING Wrong information in the story

▸ SB, pp. 122–124

a) **Read the story and cross out (~~cross out~~) SIX things that are wrong.**

| | |
|---|---|
| The people on Whitehawk estate are angry about the rubbish | |
| everywhere. So, they meet in front of the ~~library~~ at 9 a.m. on a | youth centre |
| Sunday for a clean-up day. Lily, Noah, Sunita and Zane are | |
| there. And Lily's sister Chloe and ~~Sunita's~~ dog Buddy are also | Noah's |
| there. The people put the rubbish in big rubbish ~~bins~~, but put | bags |
| things for the Swap Place in a different place. Buddy finds a | |
| lot of things, like a dead mouse, an old ~~hat~~ and a gold ring. | shoe |
| The ring has two names in it. When everybody has ~~dinner~~ | lunch |
| together, Lily tells the others about the ring. They put a note | |
| in the youth centre and ~~the next day~~ Davy phones Lily's mum | two days later |
| and tells her the ring is his grandparents' ring. | |

b) **Write the correct words on the right.**

## 17 Language in the story

▸ SB, pp. 122–124

**Complete the sentences. Use words from the box.**

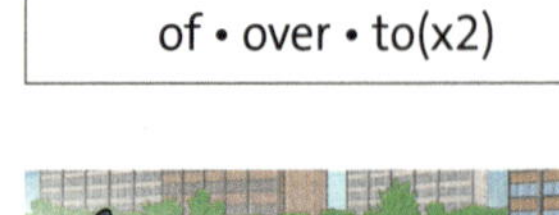
about • at • for • of • over • to(x2)

1. There's a big group of people in front *of* the youth centre.
2. A lot of people are angry *about* the rubbish everywhere.
3. "Let's put things for the Swap Place *over* there," says Olga.
4. "Let's meet here *at* 12 o'clock for lunch," says Olga.
5. Noah's dog Buddy wants *to* help.
6. Buddy digs in the ground *for* a long time.
7. People take the good things *to* the Swap Place garage.

## ☒ 18 Wrong word

**Which word is wrong? Why?**
**Use words from the box.**

activity • building • head • person • place outside • weather

1 woman grandson mouse tourist *mouse* is wrong, because it isn't a *person*.

2 busy rainy sunny cloudy *busy* because it isn't about the *weather*.

3 hospital museum field cinema *field* because it isn't a *building*.

4 buy visit travel need *need* because it isn't an *activity*.

5 bus stop street skatepark shop *shop* because it isn't a *place outside*.

6 run smell hear eat *run* because you don't do it in your *head*.

## 19 Useful presentation phrases

**Find the words. Then complete the sentences.**

1 OTAUB My presentation is *about* my town.

2 STIH In *this* photo you can see a busy street in my town.

3 TELS' *Let's* look at this photo of my favourite cafe.

4 NAY Do you have *any* questions?

5 REOM Please speak *more* loudly.

6 STAF Don't speak so *fast*, please.

7 TLINESING Thank you for *listening*.

## 20 Listening and Speaking Speak English well

20 **a) Listen to these *yes/no*-questions.**

Can you hear it? In *yes/no*-questions, the intonation goes up at the end of the sentence.

1 Do you like cooking?

2 Is it sunny today?

3 Does your town have a swimming pool?

4 Do you often eat chips?

5 Do you sometimes try new sports?

21 **b) Listen and repeat the sentences.**

**c) Say the questions in a).**
**Your partner answers. Then swap roles.**

*Do you like cooking?* *Yes, I do.* *No, I don't.*

**Three favourite words:**

(rubbish)

(chips)

(snowy)

**Three difficult words:**

(neighbourhood)

(hospital)

(mouse/mice)

**Three favourite phrases:**

(Excuse me, ...)

(You're welcome!)

(every 30 minutes)

**My favourite page in Unit 4:**

(page 125)

**Why:**

(The film is funny.)

**I remember:**

Places in town: (supermarket, library, museum, youth centre, hospital, swimming pool, ice rink, stadium, ...)

Weather words: (sunny, rainy, windy, cloudy, snowy, warm, cold)

A negative sentence with *doesn't* or *don't*: (We don't sing.)

A question with *do* or *does*: (Do you speak English?)

Five question words: when?, (how many? where? what? why?)

Where things are: behind, (in front of, inside, outside, under, over there)

**I think English is:**

☐ not hard ☐ quite hard ☐ very hard

This is quite difficult:

☐ writing words ☐ saying words

☐ learning words ☐ using verbs

*What can you do? You can practise more. You can ask the teacher or a friend for help.*

## Early finisher 1 Word puzzles

a) **Write the places in the puzzle.**

1 You can watch films here.
2 Kids can do skateboarding here.
3 A place for sport on ice.
4 A (very) small park, often behind a house.
5 You can play or sit in the sun here, next to the sea.
6 A place with computers and a lot of books.
7 A very, very big place with a lot of big and small shops and cafes.
8 This place has activities for teenagers.
9 A place where you can buy food and sometimes other things.
10 A building, or part of a building, where you can buy things like clothes.
11 Trains stop at the train ...
12 A place for people when they are not well.
13 You can watch football or other sports here.

| | | | | | | | | | | | | | | | | | | | |
|---|---|---|---|---|---|---|---|---|---|---|---|---|---|---|---|---|---|---|---|
| 1 | | | | | | C | I | N | E | M | A | | | | | | | | |
| 2 | | | | S | K | A | T | E | P | A | R | K | | | | | | | |
| 3 | | | | | | | | I | C | E | R | I | N | K | | | | | |
| 4 | | | | | | | | G | A | R | D | E | N | | | | | | |
| 5 | | | | B | E | A | C | H | | | | | | | | | | | |
| 6 | | | | | | L | I | B | R | A | R | Y | | | | | | | |
| 7 | | | | | | S | H | O | P | P | I | N | G | C | E | N | T | R | E |
| 8 | | | | | | Y | O | U | T | H | C | E | N | T | R | E | | | |
| 9 | S | U | P | E | R | M | A | R | K | E | T | | | | | | | | |
| 10 | | | | | | | S | H | O | P | | | | | | | | | |
| 11 | | | S | T | A | T | I | O | N | | | | | | | | | | |
| 12 | | | | | | | H | O | S | P | I | T | A | L | | | | | |
| 13 | | | | | S | T | A | D | I | U | M | | | | | | | | |

b) **What does the word in blue mean? Tick (✓) the correct sentence.**

1 The people who live next to you. ☐
2 The town or village where you live. ☐
3 The part of the town or village where you live. ☑

c) **Now make your own word puzzle.**
- **First, write your blue word – seven letters or more.**
- **Now choose the other words. Make one copy of the puzzle with words, and one with no words.**
- **Write sentences to explain your words, or draw pictures or symbols for your words.**

d) **Show your puzzle with no words to a partner. Can your partner complete your puzzle?**

## 18 More help 4 LISTENING Our neighbourhoods

▶WB, p. 57 ▶SB, p. 113

a) **Five students in class 7C talk about their neighbourhoods. Listen and read the texts.**

**Fatima** *Hi, my name is Fatima, and I live in a village outside Brighton. It's a nice place to live. I can often go walking in the fields with my mum and dad. I like that. And we have two shops in the village, where we can buy food. So yeah, I like where I live. The people here are friendly.*

**Finley** *OK, I'm Finley and live on an estate in Brighton. It's OK, we have a good youth centre with cool activities. I like going there. Sometimes it's loud where we live – cars go too fast, and people have loud music. But not always. It's OK.*

**Hannah** *Hi, I'm Hannah, and I live in a flat in the centre of Brighton. We have a lot of shops near us. That's great, but I don't really like it here. The streets are really dirty, and there's a lot of rubbish in the park. I don't know why people can't take their rubbish home! But they don't, so we need more bins!*

**Ivy** *So, I'm Ivy, and I live with my mum and my brother (and my dog!) on an estate in Brighton. We live in a flat on the top floor. It's OK, we have shops. And we're lucky, we're near some nice fields where I can go walking with my dog. But, well, you can't do much here really, so it can be boring here ... sometimes ...*

**Syed** *Hi, my name is Syed, and like Ivy I live on an estate, and I like it here. My friends live here, and we can play in the sports fields – we have some really nice big sports fields on the estate where we can play football and things. It's good to live here.*

b) **You choose: Listen again or listen and read. What do the students talk about? Put a tick (✓) in the right boxes.**

| | estate | shops | youth centre | fields | noise | rubbish |
|---|---|---|---|---|---|---|
| Fatima | | ✓ | | ✓ | | |
| Finley | ✓ | | ✓ | | ✓ | |
| Hannah | | ✓ | | | | ✓ |
| Ivy | ✓ | ✓ | | ✓ | | |
| Syed | ✓ | | | ✓ | | |

c) **Listen again and (circle) the right words. Then check in the text in a).**

1 Fatima says the people in her neighbourhood are (**friendly**) / **unfriendly**.

2 Finley says there is a lot of (**noise**) / **rubbish** in his neighbourhood.

3 Hannah says the streets in her neighbourhood are **clean** / (**dirty**).

4 Ivy says her neighbourhood is **interesting** / (**boring**).

5 Syed says there are some (**big**) / **small** sports fields on his estate.

Erklär-film More help

## 14 c) LANGUAGE Simple present: *wh*-questions

▶ WB, p. 63 ▶ SB, p. 121

**Write the questions.**

Use a question word: *how, what, when, where, why* + *does* or *do*. Look at the answers to find the right verb for the question.

1 Where does Kevin work ?
– He works at Thorpe Park.

2 What does Kevin do ?
– He helps the visitors.

3 How fast do visitors travel on *Stealth*? – They travel at 80 miles per hour.

4 How do visitors travel on *Vortex*? – They travel upside down.

5 When does Kevin go to work? – He goes to work at 6.45.

6 Why does Kevin like his job? – Because he can sometimes go on *Stealth* and *Vortex*.

Challenge 1

## WRITING FAQs about your neighbourhood

▶ Digital help ▶ SB, p. 63

**Write some FAQs for an online brochure about your neighbourhood for students from another country. You can write in your exercise book or here.**

FAQs are questions that people often ask – together with answers.

**You can be positive:**

- Does your town have lots of activities for 11–14 year olds?
  *Yes, it does. We have a great stadium with a lot of different sports.*
- Where do students meet after school?
  *They meet in the town centre.*

**Or you can be negative:**

- Does your town have lots of activities for 11–14 year olds?
  *No, it doesn't. We don't have a lot of youth centres.*
- Are the buses expensive?
  *Yes, they are. Very expensive!*

Four questions – OK!
Six questions – good!
Eight questions – great!

# Unit 5
# Enjoy

## 1 Lots of food

▸ SB, p. 141

a) Look at the letters. Write the words.

| | | | | | | | |
|---|---|---|---|---|---|---|---|
| 1 | tema | meat | F | 6 | tuirf | fruit | A |
| 2 | ecri | rice | E | 7 | mototа | tomato | I |
| 3 | sepa | peas | H | 8 | sechee | cheese | B |
| 4 | rebda | bread | J | 9 | sutcrad | custard | C |
| 5 | lelyj | jelly | D | 10 | tegevalbes | vegetables | G |

b) Match the pictures A–J with the correct words in a). Write the letters in the boxes.

## 2 LISTENING Lunch at school

22

▸ More help, p. 82 ▸ SB, p. 141

Oscar isn't happy. Listen and complete his sentences.

Be ready. Read the text before you listen.

Mum usually gives me (1) a cheese sandwich for lunch on school days. But I don't want that! I want to have (2) a burger in the school canteen like my friends – with (3) chips ! She always puts (4) fruit in my bag too because it's healthy. I like (5) oranges – they're OK. But I really want to have (6) chocolate ! It isn't fair!

I can talk about food.

## 3 Party invitations

► SB, p. 143

When is (___)'s party?
What time does it start?
Where is the party?
What activities are there?

Partner B: Look at page 87.
Partner A:
Ask partner B about parties 1 and 3 and write the answers.
Answer partner B's questions about parties 2 and 4.

1 **COME TO AMBER'S BIRTHDAY PARTY!**

When? Saturday 4th June
What time? At 7.30 p.m.
Where? At the youth centre
What? Dancing

2 **COME TO BEN'S SUMMER PARTY!**

When? Sunday 7th July
What time? At 12 o'clock
Where? At the beach
What? A barbecue

3 **COME TO MOLLY AND ANNA'S PARTY!**

When? Friday 1st March
What time? At 7 p.m.
Where? At Anna's house
What? Great party games

4 **COME TO HAMID'S BIRTHDAY PARTY!**

When? Monday 2nd January
What time? At 2.30 p.m.
Where? At the sports centre
What? Trampolining

## 4 LISTENING Can you come to my party?

23

► SB, p. 143

a) Listen to six people. Can they come to Ben's party? Write ✓ or ✗.

b) Listen again and look at the pictures (A–F). Write the letters in the boxes.

1 Molly ✓ E    2 Hamid ✗ A    3 Chang ✓ D
4 Anna ✗ B    5 Amber ✗ C    6 Uncle Tim ✓ F

A

B

C

D

E

F

## 5 LANGUAGE Present progressive Oscar's message to Ling

Erklärfilm

▶ SB, p. 145

Complete the message with: *'m / is / 's / are / 're*.

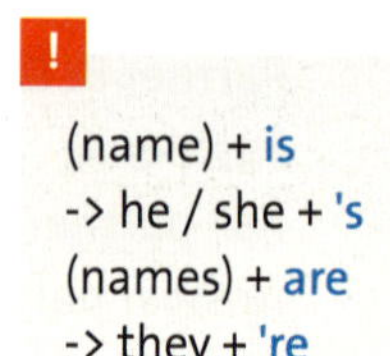

!

(name) + is
-> he / she + 's
(names) + are
-> they + 're

*Hi Ling*

*Mum and my stepdad Kevin* are *(1) sitting in the living room at the moment. They*'re *(2) watching a really stupid film. They think I*'m *(3) doing my homework, but I*'m *(4) playing on my computer (shhhh!). Freddie* is *(5) staying with his friend and Olivia isn't here – she*'s *(6) playing at a friend's house – so it's quiet ;-). What* are *(7) you doing?*

## 6 LANGUAGE Present progressive Who is doing what?

▶ SB, p. 145

Write sentences. Use the present progressive (*-ing* form).

Amber is texting her friend.
Anna is having a shower.
Hamid is juggling.
Ling's cat is sleeping on the sofa.
Molly is making lunch.

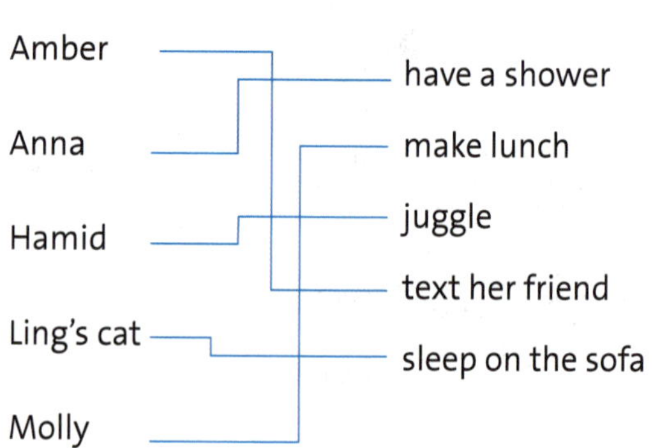

| Amber | have a shower |
|---|---|
| Anna | make lunch |
| Hamid | juggle |
| Ling's cat | text her friend |
| Molly | sleep on the sofa |

## 7 LANGUAGE Present progressive What is the girl doing?

▶ SB, p. 145

a) Look at the pictures. Write what you think the girl is doing.

▶ More help, p. 82

1  2  3

4  5  6 

1 She's playing (the) guitar.
2 She's taking photos / a photo.
3 She's listening to music.
4 She's eating something.
5 She's cleaning (her room).
6 She's brushing her teeth.

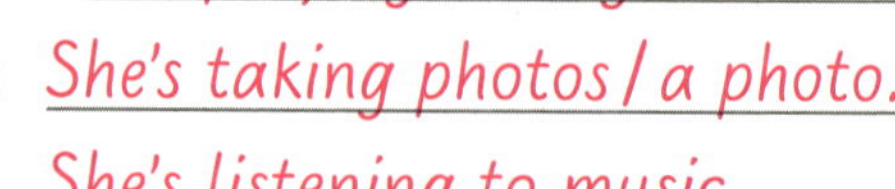

b) Mime an action. Your partner guesses what it is.

*I think you're eating an orange.*

*No, I'm eating an apple.*

## 8 LANGUAGE Present progressive It's Saturday afternoon

▸ SB, p. 145

a) Ling's mum isn't at home. There's a note for Ling – but when her mum phones, Ling *isn't* doing what her mum wants. Write what Ling *isn't* doing.

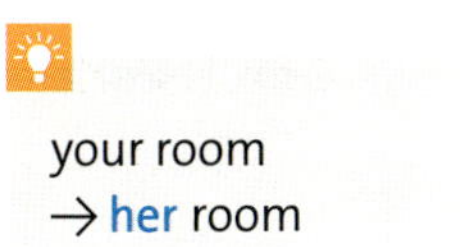


*Ling – please do these things:*
*– brush the cat*
*– tidy your room*
*– do your homework*
*– buy fruit at the shop*
*– clean the toilet*
*Mum xx*

1 *Ling isn't brushing the cat.*
2 *She isn't tidying her room.*
3 *She isn't doing her homework.*
4 *She isn't buying fruit at the shop.*
5 *She isn't cleaning the toilet.*

b) Ling's mum phones. Complete Ling's answer.

! plan → planning

*Ling, are you doing the things in my note?*

*Oh, OK – great idea!*

*Sorry, Mum. I* 'm not doing (1 not do) *those things, and I* 'm not looking (2 not look) *at your note! I* 'm making (3 make) *a birthday cake for Grandma and I* 'm planning (4 plan) *a party!*

## 9 LANGUAGE Present progressive What is happening in the photos?

▸ SB, p. 145

**Ling is showing Oscar photos from her grandma's party. Complete the sentences.**

Look at these photos, Oscar. In this photo, we 're playing (1 play) a game. Well, my brother isn't playing (2 not play) of course – he 's taking (3 take) the photo! And here, my parents are dancing (4 dance) together. But they aren't dancing (5 not dance) very well! They're so funny! And in this photo Grandma is eating (6 eat) and Kitty the cat is watching (7 watch) her – Kitty is hungry!

– What are you doing (8 do) in this photo, Ling?

– I 'm singing (9 sing) karaoke, but the others aren't listening (10 not listen). Maybe because I 'm not singing (11 not sing) a very good song!

▸ Early finisher 1, p. 81 ▸ Challenge 1, p. 82

I can talk about birthdays and parties.

## 10 A birthday present

▸ SB, p. 146

**Ling, Oscar and Hamid are talking about Amber's birthday. Complete the sentences.**

| about • already • don't • idea • perfect • present • sure |
|---|

**Ling** Let's buy a *present* for Amber. It's her party soon.

**Hamid** That's a good *idea*, Ling. I know! Why *don't* we buy a sweatshirt?

**Oscar** Mmm... I'm not *sure* – they're quite expensive.

**Ling** And Amber *already* has lots of sweatshirts. What *about* a smart hat?

**Hamid** That's *perfect*! Let's look online.

## 11 A thank you email

▸ SB, p. 146

a) READING **Read Amber's thank you email and look at the pictures. Tick (✓) all the presents from her grandparents.**

to grandparents55@example.com
from contactamber@example.com

Dear Grandma and Grandpa

Thank you very much for the money and the juggling balls. I really like them. They're a great present because I love circuses and I'm learning to do circus tricks.

Amber xx

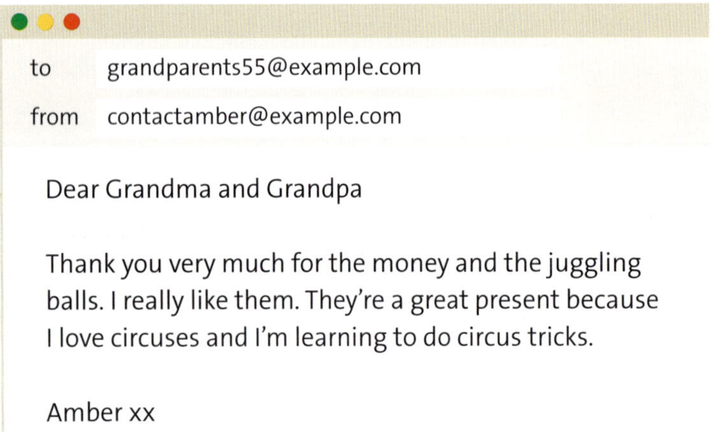

A ☐

B ☑

C ☐

D ☑

b) WRITING **Now write Amber's email to Uncle Matt.**

▸ More help, p. 83

*presents*: music books *Amber loves*: music
*she's learning to*: play the guitar

Use phrases from the email in a).

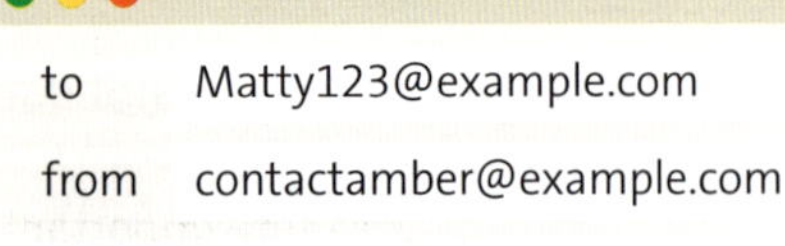

to Matty123@example.com
from contactamber@example.com

*Dear Uncle Matt*

*Thank you very much for the music books. I really like them. They're a great present because I love music and I'm learning to play the guitar.*

*Amber xx*

## 12 LANGUAGE *much, many, a lot* Things for a party

Erklär-film

▶ SB, p. 147

Partner B: Look at page 87.
Partner A: Look at the list and the pictures.
Talk with partner B about the things on the list:
ask questions and answer B's questions.
Write the answers on the list. You start.

| Questions | Answers |
|---|---|
| *How much ... is there?* | *Not much. /* |
| *How many ... are there?* | *Not many. / A lot.* |

1 2 3

4 5

| | |
|---|---|
| sausages | not many |
| bread | not much |
| cheese | a lot |
| carrots | a lot |
| salad | not much |
| ham | a lot |
| strawberries | not many |
| milk | not much |
| lemonade | a lot |
| tomatoes | not many |

## 13 LANGUAGE *much, many, a lot of* Amber's party

▶ SB, p. 148

a) Uncle Matt asks Amber about her party.
Circle the correct words.

**Uncle** How **many** / much people are coming to your party, Amber?

**Amber** Oh, it's a big party – much / **a lot of** friends are coming.

**Uncle** How a lot of / **much** time do you have before the party?

**Amber** Not many / **much** – it's at 7.30. And there are **a lot of** / much things to do! Mum is making many / **a lot of** food, but we don't have many / **much** cola. And the hall at the youth centre must look nice – but we don't have **many** / much balloons...

**Uncle** It's OK, I can go to the shops for you. How **many** / much things do you need?

**Amber** Oh thanks, Uncle Matt! Mum can make a shopping list for you.

!
*Much / many / a lot of:*
Die Regel gilt nicht nur für Essen.

b) Tell a partner about your perfect party.
What things are / aren't important?

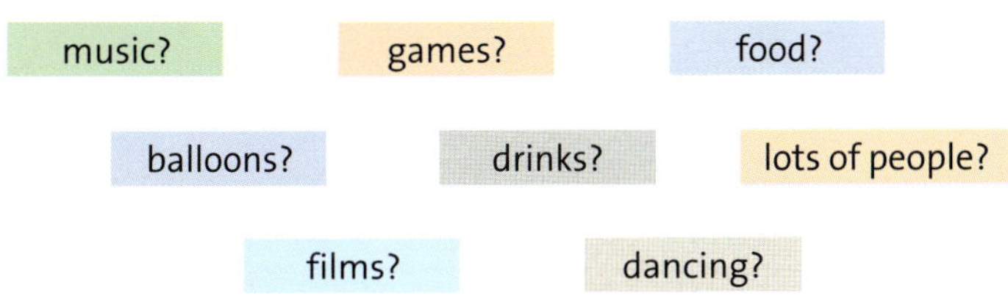


My perfect party has ...
... is / are quite important, too.
But ... isn't / aren't important.
What about you?

▶ Early finisher 2, p. 81

I can talk about party food and activities 

## 14 Ling is making a carrot cake

▶ SB, p. 150

**a)** Look at the pictures and write the correct words from the list.

Carrot cake

230 g grated[1] carrot
2 eggs
120 ml oil
160 g sugar
1 teaspoon vanilla
230 g flour
1 teaspoon baking powder
1 teaspoon cinnamon[2]
¼ teaspoon salt

100 g icing sugar
50 g butter
200 g cream cheese[3]

1 eggs
2 butter
3 salt
4 flour
5 oil
6 teaspoon

**b)** Find the words and complete the sentences.

| | | Picture |
|---|---|---|
| barekgin | 1 Ling is breaking the eggs. | B |
| mingxi | 2 She's mixing the eggs with the carrot, oil, sugar and vanilla. | E |
| angdid | 3 She's adding the flour, baking powder, salt and cinnamon. | D |
| pugtint | 4 She's putting the mixture into the oven (190° for 40–50 minutes). | F |
| magnik | 5 She's making the icing with icing sugar, butter and cream cheese. | C |
| dorecitang | 6 She's decorating the cake with icing. | A |

**c)** Match the pictures A–F with the sentences 1–6 in b). Write the letters in the boxes.

[1] **grated** *gerieben* [2] **cinnamon** *Zimt* [3] **cream cheese** *Frischkäse (Doppelrahmstufe)*

## 15 Mediation **Delicious**

▸ SB, p. 151

Your friend sends you a message with a link to a website: My favourite dish. She asks you about chocolate trifle. Write back and answer her questions.

**Harry**

*Hi everybody! My favourite dish is a dessert my grandma makes – it's chocolate trifle. It's a special dish for me, because grandma always makes it for my birthday. She makes it with pieces of cake, fruit and fruit juice[1] and pieces of chocolate. Then she makes custard with cocoa and puts that on the trifle, and after that she decorates it with cream and more little pieces of chocolate. Yum – it's delicious!*

1 Warum ist *chocolate trifle* etwas Besonderes für Harry?

Seine Oma macht es immer zu seinem Geburtstag.

2 Ich habe von *trifle* gehört, aber woraus bestehen die Schichten des *chocolate trifle*?

aus Kuchenstücken, Obst, (Frucht-)Saft,

Schokoladenstücken und Vanillesoße mit Kakao

3 Und womit wird es dekoriert?

mit Sahne und kleinen Schokoladenstücken

## 16 **What is in your favourite dish?**

▸ More help, p. 83 ▸ SB, p. 151

24

a) Listening **Listen to three people. Write four things in each person's favourite dish.**

| 1 Hazel – a British dish | 2 Ellis – Chinese stir-fry | 3 Marta – chilli con carne |
|---|---|---|
| fish | chicken | meat |
| chips | onions | tomato sauce |
| peas | peppers | spices |
| curry sauce | noodles | rice |

b) **You can eat one of the dishes in exercises 15 and 16 a). Which dish do you choose, and why?**

I choose: ______________________

because: ______________________

______________________

*Hmmm, yum!*

[1] **fruit juice** *(Frucht-)Saft*

## 17 VIEWING Watch and learn

► SB, p.155

***Watching*** **the video can help you understand new words. Tick (✓) and write the correct answers.**

**Part 1 (00:37 to 01:09)** *Watch* Emir when he says "**A hundred percent**[1]"

What does he mean? A [✓] Yes, I *really* want to come. B [ ] Mmm... Maybe...

**Parts 5 & 6 (04:17 to 05:31)** *Watch* what they buy. Write the German words:

**candles** = Kerzen **a banner** = Girlande **napkins** = Servietten

## 18 VIEWING You can act

► SB, p.155

a) **Watch Part 2 (01:10 to 02:10) again and read the script. Listen to *how* they say the sentences.**

**Daisy** Is that for Gloria?

**Emir** Yes.

**Daisy** Here. A list – for tomorrow.

**Emir** Birthday cake, candles, balloons, ...and how about[2] a birthday dare?

**Daisy** Hmm... A birthday dare? Yes. Why not? Give me a pen. Quick! And that's for you...

**Emir** You are sooo bad!

**Daisy** So... let's do it?

b) **Practise saying the sentences with a partner. Partner A is Daisy, partner B is Emir.**

c) **Now play the video with no sound. You and your partner say the words for Daisy and Emir. Do it lots of times so you're really good.**

You can watch again and copy *how* Daisy and Emir say the sentences.

## 19 VIEWING Daisy's imaginary[3] friend

► SB, p.155

**Watch Part 3 (02:11 to 03:06): Listen to what Daisy says to her imaginary friend, Sota. What do you think Sota says to her? Tick (✓) the correct answer.**

1 a) [ ] Please. b) [✓] Thanks.

2 a) [✓] I'm good. Are you? b) [ ] I'm tired after the journey.

3 a) [✓] When is the party? b) [ ] Where is the party?

4 a) [ ] But I don't know Gloria. b) [✓] But I don't have a present for Gloria.

[1] **percent** *Prozent* [2] **how about ...? = what about ...?** [3] **imaginary** *Fantasie-, vorgestellt*

## 20 It's a kind of...

a) The letters *a, e, i, o, u* are missing in these words. Write the words correctly – in the right groups.

b-n-n- c-rr-t ch-ck-n c-ff-- h-m l-m-n m-l-n -n--n p-pp-r p-t-t- s--s-g- str-wb-rry t-- w-t-r

| It's a kind of fruit | It's a kind of meat | It's a kind of drink | It's a kind of vegetable |
|---|---|---|---|
| banana | chicken | coffee | carrot |
| lemon | ham | tea | onion |
| melon | sausage | water | pepper |
| strawberry | | | potato |

b) Write at least five more food words – things that are not fruit, meat, drinks or vegetables!

▸ Digital help

(butter, cheese, cream, custard, egg, fish, flour, noodles, oil, pasta, rice, salt, spaghetti, sugar, ...)

## 21 Listening Ling's food quiz

25 a) Ling is describing food. Listen and write the food.

1 banana 2 custard 3 pea

4 egg 5 cheese 6 tomato

26 b) Listen and check your answers.

## 27 22 Listening and Speaking Speak English well

a) How do you say the *s* at the end of the word? Listen to the words and sentences and write *s* or *z*.

potatoes – z strawberries – z carrots – s melons – z

chips – s lemons – z noodles – z cakes – s

bananas – z spoons – z forks – s packets – s

*After the sounds **p**, **t**, **c/k** and **th**, you say **s**.*

b) Listen again and repeat the words and sentences.

**Three favourite words:**

(magic)

(wok)

(party)

| Three difficult words: | to write | to say |
|---|---|---|
| (healthy) | ☐ | ☐ |
| (delicious) | ☐ | ☐ |
| (knife) | ☐ | ☐ |

## I remember:

Twelve months: January, February, March, April, May, June, July, August, September, October, November, December

Some things to eat and drink: (bananas, cheese, cream, custard, eggs, fish, ham, noodles, potatoes, rice, spaghetti, ...)

Some party things: (balloons, dancing, food, games, music, ...)

How to talk about buying birthday presents: **Complete these sentences.**

Let's buy a present for Ling. What about a T-shirt? Why don't we buy a book?

How to say what someone is / isn't doing: **Write three sentences.**

Scout – not fly / talk / take a photo

Scout isn't flying.

She's talking.

She's taking a photo.

## English and me:

| For me: | usually easy | quite hard / sometimes hard | usually hard |
|---|---|---|---|
| listening exercises are... | | | |
| reading exercises are... | | | |
| writing words is... | | | |
| saying words is... | | | |
| learning words is... | | | |
| using verbs is... | | | |

*Ask a friend to test you on the words in your VOCAB FILE. Practise the difficult words. That helps with listening, reading and writing!*

**Early finisher 1** 
## Word snake puzzle

**Find the words. Each word starts with the last letter of the last word. These letters are in blue.**

**Example:** M ___ Y ___ ___ R ___ ___ E ___ ___ ___ T   MAYEARICEIGHT

1 Noah's birthday party is a ________ party.
2 My favourite present is a magic ________.
3 I love doing magic ________!
4 Summer is a hot ________.
5 The eleventh month.
6 I'm tired. I want to ________.
7 Phone or ________ if you can come to my party.
8 3rd
9 Christmas ________ is the 25th December.
10 The colour of custard.

**Early finisher 2** 
## Can you find the differences?

**Find eight differences and write what they are.**

the girl is ...ing
it's ...

| In picture A ... | but in picture B ... |
|---|---|
| the people are *eating chips,* | they're *eating potatoes.* |
| *the cat is sleeping,* | *the cat is sitting.* |
| *the girl is wearing a hat,* | *she isn't wearing a hat.* |
| *they're drinking water,* | *they're drinking milk.* |
| *it's 6 o'clock,* | *it's 6.30 p.m.* |
| *it's spring,* | *it's autumn.* |
| *it's sunny,* | *it's rainy.* |
| *it's Sunday,* | *it's Monday.* |

▸ Check

## More help 2 LANGUAGE Lunch at school

22

▶ WB, p. 70 ▶ SB, p. 141

**Oscar isn't happy. Listen and (circle) the right words.**

Mum usually gives me a (cheese) / big / nice sandwich for lunch on school days. But I don't want that!

I want to have lunch / pizza / (a burger) in the school canteen like my friends – with cola / hot chocolate / (chips)! She always puts water / (fruit) / vegan food in my bag too because it's healthy. I like strawberries / (oranges) / apples – they're OK. But I really want to have (chocolate) / sweets / other things too! It isn't fair!

## More help 7 LANGUAGE What is the girl doing?

▶ WB, p. 72 ▶ SB, p. 141

a) **Look at the pictures. Write what you think the girl is doing.**

| brushing • cleaning • eating • listening • playing • taking |
|---|

| the guitar • to music • a photo • her room • something • her teeth |
|---|

1 
2 
3 
4 
5 
6 

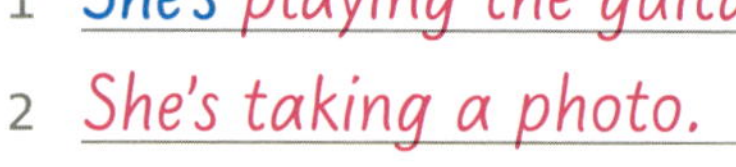

1 *She's playing the guitar.*
2 *She's taking a photo.*
3 *She's listening to music.*
4 *She's eating something.*
5 *She's cleaning her room.*
6 *She's brushing her teeth.*

## Challenge 1 Questions to Ling

▶ WB, p. 73

a) **It's the morning of Grandma's party. Write the questions.**

| | | Answers to b): |
|---|---|---|
| 1 Where / you / go, Ling? | *Where are you going, Ling?* | D |
| 2 Why / you / buy / balloons? | *Why are you buying balloons?* | F |
| 3 What / you / write? | *What are you writing?* | B |
| 4 What / your big brother / do? | *What is your big brother doing?* | A |
| 5 Why / he / make / trifle? | *Why is he making trifle?* | E |
| 6 What / your parents / do? | *What are your parents doing?* | C |

b) Find the answers and write the letters next to the correct questions on page 82. ▸ Check

**Answers:**

A *He's making trifle.*

B *A birthday card for my grandma.*

C *They're cleaning the house.*

D *To the shops.*

E *Because it's Grandma's favourite dessert!*

F *They're for Grandma's party.*

## ☒ More help 11 A thank you message

▸ WB, p. 74 ▸ SB, p. 146

b) WRITING **Now write Amber's message to Uncle Matt.**

*presents*: music books *Amber loves*: music
*she's learning to*: play the guitar

Dear...
Thank you very much for the...
I really like them.
They're a great present because I love ...
and I'm learning to ...

to Matty123@example.com
from contactamber@example.com

Dear Uncle Matt

Thank you very much for the music books. I really like them. They're a great present because I love music and I'm learning to play the guitar.

Amber xx

## More help 16 LISTENING What is in your favourite dish?

▸ WB, p. 77 ▸ SB, p. 151

24

a) Listen to three people. Tick (✓) four things in each person's favourite dish.

1 Hazel – a British dish

- [x] chips
- [ ] carrots
- [x] curry sauce
- [ ] tomato sauce
- [x] fish
- [x] peas

2 Ellis – Chinese stir-fry

- [x] noodles
- [x] onions
- [ ] rice
- [x] peppers
- [x] chicken
- [ ] ham

3 Marta – chilli con carne

- [x] tomato sauce
- [ ] cheese
- [x] spices
- [x] meat
- [ ] potatoes
- [x] rice

## 1 Tia's house

**Write the names of the rooms.**

bathroom • bedroom • dining room • hall • kitchen • living room • office • toilet

1 
kitchen

2 
living room

3 
bathroom

4 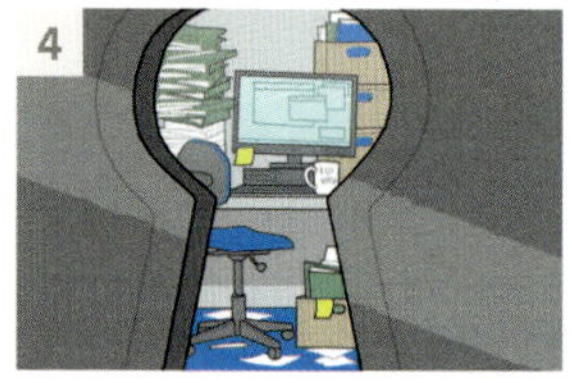
office

5 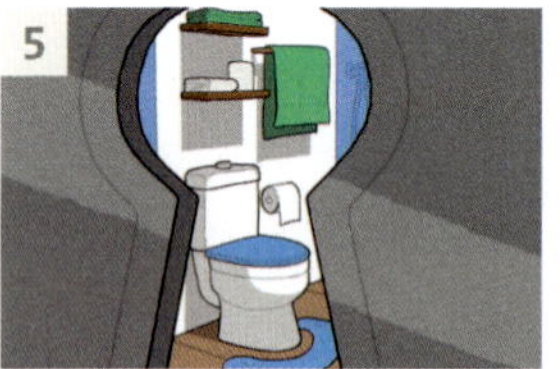
toilet

6 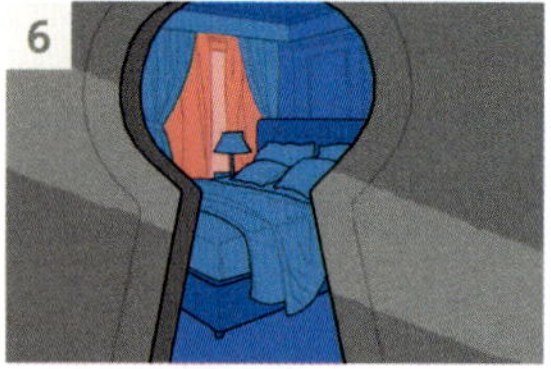
bedroom

7 
hall

8 
dining room

## 2 Tia's family

**Complete the sentences. Write the letters in the boxes.**

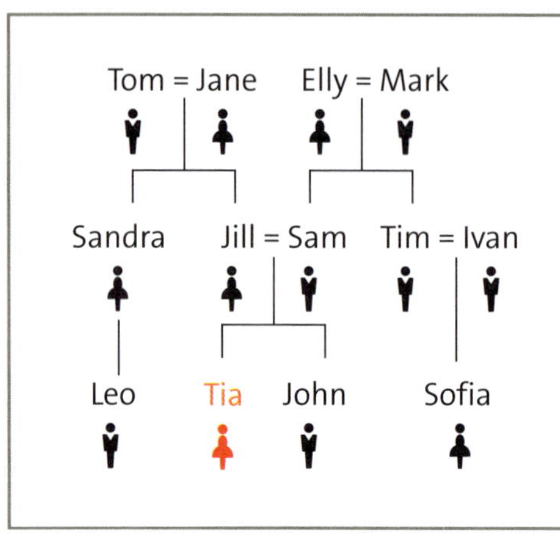


1 John is Tia's... C
2 Jill is Tom and Jane's... A
3 Tim is Ivan's... D
4 Elly and Mark are Tia's... B
5 Tia is Leo's... F
6 Leo is Tom and Jane's... G
7 Sandra is Tia and John's... E

A daughter.
B grandparents.
C brother.
D husband.
E aunt.
F cousin.
G grandson.

## 3 Tia talks about her family

**Write the correct words:** *my / your / his / her / our / their*.

*Tom and Jane are* my *grandparents. They live near here, at* their *daughter Sandra's house. Aunt Sandra is really nice.* Her *son, Leo, comes here on Saturdays. He often brings* his *friend, Ali, and we all play on* our *bikes. What about you? Tell me about* your *family.*

► Check

Erklär-
film

## 4 Tia talks to her friend Oscar

▶ Digital help

**Complete the sentences. Use the simple present.**

**Tia** (1 What / you / do) What do you do at the weekend, Oscar?

**Oscar** I (2 go) go to football training every Saturday morning. My little sister (3 like) likes the park, so we (4 play) play games there together in the afternoon. My parents (5 not come) don't come – they're too busy. (6 you / go) Do you go to the park, Tia?

**Tia** Yes, I do, but I (7 not go) don't go there very often. My favourite place is the swimming pool. My uncle Tim (8 take) takes me and my cousin there every Sunday. He (9 not like) doesn't like swimming, so he (10 have) has a drink in the cafe. (11 Where / you / go) Where do you go on Sunday, Oscar?

**Oscar** Mum and I sometimes (12 visit) visit my grandma, but we (13 not see) don't see her every Sunday. She always (14 give) gives me chocolate!

## 5 Tia and her friends talk about their neighbourhoods

a) **Look at the letters and read the sentences. Write the words in the right sentences.**

byus | dryti | bringo | canel | qetui | undrinefly

1 *People don't put their rubbish in the bins on my estate. The streets are* dirty.

4 *We have a shopping centre. Lots of people go there – it's always* busy.

2 *There isn't much noise in our street – it's* quiet *here.*

5 *People in my street never talk to me. They're quite* unfriendly.

3 *There are no good places for young people here. It's really* boring.

6 *We have no rubbish in our neighbourhood – it's very* clean.

b) **Write five more words you can use to talk about a neighbourhood.**

(cool, horrible, loud, friendly, modern, nice, old, ...)

▶ Check

## Unit 4 Topic 2 | Exercise 11

▸ WB, p. 61 ▸ SB, p. 117

Partner B: You want to know:
Is York a good place for a holiday in England?

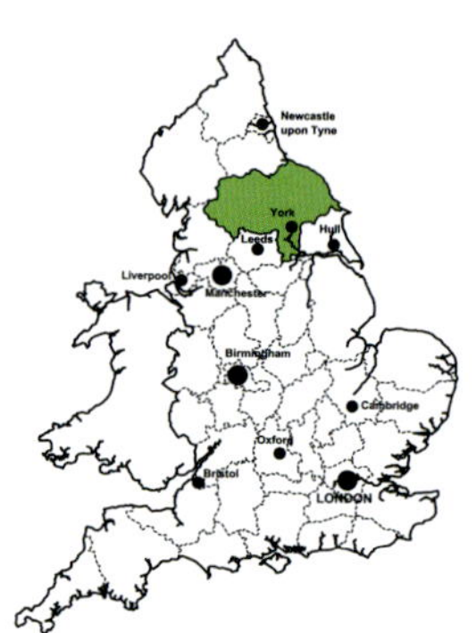


a) Write the questions about York. Put the words in the right order.

1 York / a train museum / does / have / ?
*Does York have a train museum?* ✓

2 a marina / does / or beach / have / York / ?
*Does York have a marina or a beach?* ✗

3 have / nice old streets / does / York / and buildings / ?
*Does York have nice old streets and buildings?* 

4 a big / York / football stadium / have / does / ?
*Does York have a big football stadium?* 

5 shops / does / have / York / interesting / ?
*Does York have interesting shops?* 

b) Your partner wants to know about Devon. Look at the information.

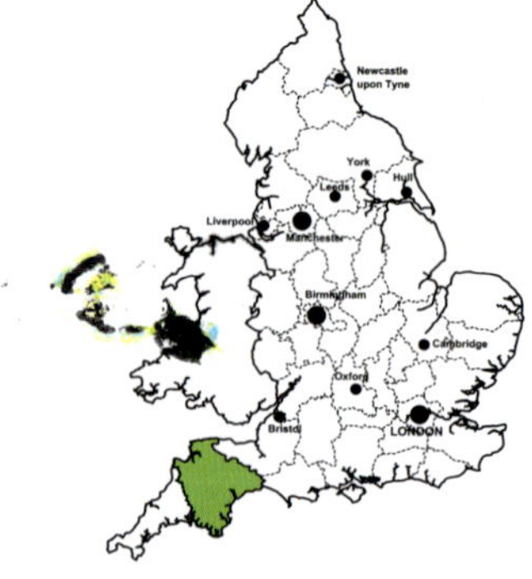


Devon has great beaches and is great for windsurfing. It also has places for good long hikes. But Devon doesn't have any good football clubs, and doesn't have many big cities.

c) Your partner asks you about Devon.
Answer your partner's questions. Use short answers: ***Yes, it does. / No, it doesn't.***

d) Now ask your questions about York. Put a tick (✓) in the box for yes, an ✗ for no.

e) Check your answers with your partner.

## Unit 5 Topic 1 | Exercise 3

▶ WB, p. 71 ▶ SB, p. 143

Partner B:
Answer partner A's questions about parties 1 and 3.
Ask partner A about parties 2 and 4 and write the answers.

When is (___)'s party?
What time does it start?
Where is the party?
What activities are there?

1

**COME TO AMBER'S BIRTHDAY PARTY!**

When? Saturday 4th June

What time? At 7.30 p.m.

Where? At the youth centre

What? Dancing

2

**COME TO BEN'S SUMMER PARTY!**

When? Sunday 7th July

What time? At 12 o'clock

Where? At the beach

What? A barbecue

3

**COME TO MOLLY AND ANNA'S PARTY!**

When? Friday 1st March

What time? At 7 p.m.

Where? At Anna's house

What? Great party games

4

**COME TO HAMID'S BIRTHDAY PARTY!**

When? Monday 2nd January

What time? At 2.30 p.m.

Where? At the sports centre

What? Trampolining

## Unit 5 Topic 2 | Exercise 12

▶ WB, p. 75 ▶ SB, p. 147

Erklär-film

Partner B: Look at the list and the pictures. Talk with partner A about the things on the list: ask questions and answer A's questions. Write the answers on the list. Partner A starts.

| Questions | Answers |
|---|---|
| *How much ... is there?* | *Not much. /* |
| *How many ... are there?* | *Not many. / A lot.* |

1 2 3

4 5

| | |
|---|---|
| sausages | not many |
| bread | not much |
| cheese | a lot |
| carrots | a lot |
| salad | not much |
| ham | a lot |
| strawberries | not many |
| milk | not much |
| lemonade | a lot |
| tomatoes | not many |

| Typical tasks | Häufige Arbeitsanweisungen |
| --- | --- |
| Act the conversation / part. | Führt das Gespräch / die Szene vor. |
| Answer the questions / partner B's questions. | Beantworte die Fragen / Partner/in Bs Fragen. |
| Ask questions. | Stelle Fragen. |
| Check with your partner. | Überprüfe mit deiner Partnerin / deinem Partner. |
| Choose the correct verbs / a person / ... | Wähle die richtigen Verben / eine Person / ... |
| Circle the right word / correct verb / ... | Kreise das richtige Wort / das richtige Verb / ... ein. |
| Complete the questions / message / ... | Vervollständige die Fragen / die Nachricht / ... |
| Cross out the numbers / wrong things / ... | Streiche die Nummern / die falschen Dinge / ... durch. |
| Draw pictures / lines / ... | Zeichne / Male Bilder / Linien / ... |
| Fill the gaps with the right words. | Vervollständige die Lücken mit den richtigen Wörtern. |
| Find the answers / right picture / ... | Finde die Antworten / das richtige Bild / ... |
| Highlight the letters / words / ... | Markiere die Buchstaben / Wörter / ... |
| Listen again. | Höre nochmal zu. |
| Listen and check / read / write / ... | Höre zu und überprüfe / lies / schreibe / ... |
| Listen to the words / sentences / people / ... | Höre dir die Wörter / Sätze / Leute / ... an. |
| Look at the picture / answers / ... | Schau dir das Bild / die Antwort / ... an. |
| Match the pictures / ... with the sentences / ... | Ordne die Bilder / ... den Sätzen / ... zu. |
| Practise with a partner. | Übe mit einem/r Partner/in. |
| Put a cross in the box for the wrong sentences. | Setze ein Kreuzchen ins Kästchen für die falschen Sätze. |
| Put a tick in the box for the correct sentences / in the right boxes. | Setze ein Häkchen ins Kästchen für die richtigen Sätze / in die richtigen Kästchen. |
| Put the words in the right order. | Setze die Wörter in die richtige Reihenfolge. |
| Read about ... | Lies über ... |
| Read the messages / sentences / text / ... | Lies die Nachrichten / Sätze / den Text / ... |
| Right (✓) or wrong (✗)? / True (T) or false (F)? | Richtig oder falsch? |
| Swap roles. | Wechselt die Rollen. |
| Talk to a partner. | Sprich mit einem/r Partner/in. |
| Tick the correct definition / the hobbies / ... | Hake alle richtigen Definitionen / Hobbys / ... ab. |
| Underline ... | Unterstreiche ... |
| Use the answers / letters / ... in the box. | Benutze die Antworten / Buchstaben / ... aus dem Kasten. |
| Use words from the box. | Benutze die Wörter aus dem Kasten. |
| Watch part 1/2/... (again). | Sieh dir Teil 1/2/... (nochmal) an. |
| Write about six sports / your grandma / ... | Schreibe über sechs Sportarten / deine Oma / ... |
| Write definitions / the answers / the sentences / ... | Schreibe die Definitionen / die Antworten / die Sätze / ... |

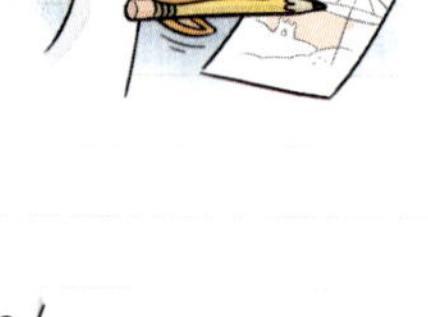